Pop Stars, Pageants & Presidents:

How An Email Trumped My Life

Two Many Hats
PUBLISHING

Rob Goldstone

Two Many Hats Publishing / Oui 2 Entertainment
www.robgoldstone.net

Connect with Rob Goldstone on social media:
🐦 @GoldstoneRob
📷 @robgoldstone
🅕 facebook.com/rgoldst

ISBN: 978-1-7326862-0-5 (hardback)
ISBN: 978-1-7326862-2-9 (paperback)
ISBN: 978-1-7326862-1-2 (ebook)

Artwork: Ann Irwin
Edit/Proofing: Barry Dougherty/Mark Hunter
Cover Design: Andrew Torrey
Jacket Photo: Fadil Berisha
Book Layout: Michelle Lovi

This book is dedicated to
H.M. King Willem-Alexander of the Netherlands.

Table of Contents

Preface   1

Chapter One • Life Interrupted   3

Chapter Two • An Unexpected Proposal   9

Chapter Three • The Elvis of Azerbaijan   15

Chapter Four • To Russia with Love   23

Chapter Five • What Happens in Vegas…   29

Chapter Six • Delicate Child   41

Chapter Seven • The Greatest   51

Chapter Eight • Down To the Wire   57

Chapter Nine • The Showman Cometh   67

Chapter Ten • The King and I   83

Chapter Eleven • London Calling   93

Chapter Twelve • The World According to Emin   99

Chapter Thirteen • A Higher Office   107

Chapter Fourteen • That Infamous Email   113

Chapter Fifteen • Bait and Switch   123

Chapter Sixteen • Hiding in Plain Sight   137

Chapter Seventeen • Meet the Muppet   153

Chapter Eighteen • Capital Punishment   163

Chapter Nineteen • 1600 Pennsylvania Avenue   177

Chapter Twenty • Mueller, Me & the Grand Jury   183

Chapter Twenty-One • Got Me Good   189

Preface

I wrote what has been called the most famous email in history.

One hundred and thirty-seven words written on a cellphone in under three minutes to the son of the future president of the United States. That email has been scrutinized, analyzed, debated, picked apart, and judged like no email ever before.

It was this email that led to the Trump Tower meeting, and it was this email that helped ignite RussiaGate and its investigations into election meddling and collusion.

And it is this email that still threatens to bring down the 45th president of the United States, Donald J. Trump.

Chapter One

Life Interrupted

It had just gone noon on Sunday, July 9, 2017. I was sitting in an outdoor taverna in Athens, in a small square surrounded by Greek plane trees for which the crowded restaurant was named, when my cellphone started to ring. In the glare of the midday sun I couldn't see who was calling but, having just spent a week on a cruise ship with spotty reception, I decided to answer it anyway.

"Hello?"

There was silence, and for a moment I thought it was a cold call or wrong number and almost hung up. But then she spoke.

"This is Rosalind Helderman from *The Washington Post*," she said.

The name was unfamiliar, but after decades of taking calls from every conceivable type of journalist, I wasn't surprised. She wasted no time and asked if I was the one who had set up the Trump Tower meeting between a Russian attorney and Donald Trump, Jr. She told me that the day before *The New York Times* had run a story about the meeting without naming the person who organized it.

"Were you the one who set it up?" she asked again.

It would have been easy enough to hang up as if the call had disconnected or just say "no comment," but this was, after all, *The Washington Post*. Besides, I knew, as any good publicist knows, that giving a "no comment" is often just a cagey way of avoiding a question.

I told her "yes," that I had set up the meeting on behalf of a client, adding that I had also attended. Although I didn't name him, the client was Russian pop star Emin Agalarov, who had requested the meeting for his billionaire father, property tycoon Aras Agalarov. I had acted as conduit between Emin and Aras and the Trumps, as I had done on previous occasions.

I tried to remember other details, but whether it was the heat or being put on the spot, the only thing that came to mind was that the attorney had talked about a ban on American adoptions of Russian children. I also remembered how she had asked if the Trump campaign could keep an eye on this issue should Donald Trump be elected, and perhaps she could have a future conversation with them about it.

Although *The Washington Post* call took me off guard, I recalled that a few weeks earlier, while I was traveling in Brazil, attorneys from the Trump Organization had reached out to me asking questions about this same meeting. They wanted to know the name of the Russian lawyer and anything else I could remember about it. Details of the meeting, they said, had leaked to the media, and one of the attorneys had specifically commented that the White House was "full of leaks."

I was completely unaware that what was unfolding would, in a few short hours, make headlines around the world. In hindsight, it's astounding how oblivious I was. So oblivious, in fact, that after lunch I went shopping and sightseeing on the way back to the hotel.

I had arrived in Athens that morning with my partner David. Although I was excited to be back in Greece after a twenty-year absence, I was even more excited to be at the start of my "gap" year. For the next nine months, I would do nothing but travel and write a book chronicling my adventures as a fifty-something "student" traveler. I'd spent years dreaming about this adventure, and now it was finally happening.

The cruise ship had docked in the port of Piraeus at around 7 a.m., and after clearing customs we made our way down the gangplank and headed straight to the InterContinental Hotel, near the city center, where we planned to spend the next three days. The early morning streets were deserted, and after a week of living on a packed cruise ship, the peace and quiet of Athens on a Sunday morning was like heaven—with church bells ringing in the background.

At check-in, I asked the hotel concierge for a recommendation for lunch, and he suggested one of his favorites and booked us a table at Platanos Taverna, in the Plaka district. We took a taxi to an area not far from the restaurant, and decided to walk the rest of the way and explore a little.

Even that early, it was already hot; the sky blue and cloudless. A week of sea air and days exploring Venice, Dubrovnik, Montenegro, and Corfu had left me relaxed and recharged.

As we neared the restaurant, we passed a sign that read "Bathhouse of the Winds," the site of the remnants of a seventeenth century Ottoman public bath. I stopped and took a picture for Facebook and Instagram and posted it with a cheeky comment about flatulence.

After lunch, we went back to exploring Plaka, through the labyrinth of cobblestone streets and jumble of artisan shops and souvenir stalls. Eventually we ended up in a small store that specialized in handmade gold leaf crowns and laurel wreaths. Never one to pass up the chance to put a crown on my head, I tried on a few and took some selfies with my iPhone. A favorite pastime of mine is taking ridiculous selfies in weird and wonderful hats. It's just something I'm known for among my friends, and I make a point of never disappointing. A gold crown was something I simply couldn't pass up...or pass by.

I joked with the shop owner that I should be her publicist and make her crowns famous. Little did I know that within a few days, a picture of me in one of her laurel wreaths would circle the globe and show up in dozens of articles and TV news reports. Never in my career had I generated so much publicity, so quickly, for someone who wasn't even a client.

By the time we got back to the hotel an hour later, calls were coming in fast and furious, and the phone in the room was ringing off the hook. *What was happening?* Aside from anything else, how did anyone know where I was? Then I remembered that I'd "checked in" on Facebook that morning after we arrived at the hotel.

I began to read through the barrage of emails, each one asking about the Trump Tower meeting and requesting an interview or comment. Something was seriously wrong, and I needed to find and speak to Emin as soon as possible. He was in Moscow and, I assumed, unaware of what was happening. My immediate priority was to get hold of him, explain what was going on so he fully understood, and get him to agree to release some kind of statement to help calm the frenzy. I texted him and included a link to *The New York Times* story.

I told him that I'd kept him and his father out of the conversation when I spoke to *The Washington Post* reporter, but that she had mentioned him by name.

"Was your client Emin Agalarov?" she had asked.

Even though I refused to confirm it, there was no doubt she knew Emin was the client. I couldn't hold back my anger at him for having put me in this situation. I rarely lost my cool with hin, but I ended the text message bluntly: "I hope this favor was worth it for your dad. It could blow up big."

A few minutes later, Emin left me a voice message trying to calm me down. "Stay cool, you have nothing to do with this. Everything you've done is just connect people."

That was easy for him to say. He lived in Moscow, in a world of privilege and protection. He would be shielded. I, however, was thousands of miles away from home, in a hotel room, in the center of a chaotic storm that was growing.

I have been a publicist for more than thirty years and before that a journalist, so I am very comfortable talking to the media. But this was a different kettle of fish. There was also the issue that I had dozens of friends all over the world who were journalists and editors, and connected to me on Facebook and Instagram. Most of them were already asking me for a comment. *How could I avoid them all?*

I decided to do two phone interviews: *The New York Times* and the Associated Press. These were key outlets and would have a broad reach both in the US and internationally. At that moment, the last thing I wanted was to speak to anyone in the press, but I knew I had to do something and this seemed like the right move. But it was only after I finished the second of those interviews that the true reality of the situation sank in.

It was turning into a full-scale political scandal, possibly the biggest in decades. And I was not just involved, I was at the heart of it. I couldn't process what was happening; everything was escalating so quickly, and seemed to be getting more out of control by the hour. When I had arrived in Athens that morning, my biggest concern had been where to have lunch. Now I was caught in a typhoon that stretched from the White House to the Kremlin.

A few hours later, two of my closest friends in New York called to see if I was OK. They said my picture was on every television channel and all over the internet. They asked if I had spoken to a lawyer. *Why would I need to speak to a lawyer?* Except for the closing on my mortgage, I hadn't used one in years. They eventually convinced me that this situation was serious enough for me to find an attorney who could guide me through what would turn out to be the most challenging year of my life.

And to think, it all began with a beauty pageant.

Chapter 2

An Unexpected Proposal

Growing up in Manchester, in northern England, two yearly events were sacrosanct in my household: the Eurovision Song Contest and the Miss World beauty pageant. The first was a Eurocentric battle of kitschy pop songs, while the second was an extravaganza of international beauties that brought campy escapism to Britain's mostly gray skies.

The Miss World contest, in particular, had special meaning for my family. Each year during the show my mother would repeat the same story of how she had once danced with the pageant's founder Eric Morley at the Ritz Ballroom in Manchester. She was convinced that had she been a bit lighter on her feet in the quickstep, she might have ended up as Mrs. Morley and gone on to become the queen of beauty pageants. That role was ultimately taken by Julia Morley, who still holds the position today.

So I can only imagine how excited my mother would have been when, in 2013, I found myself involved in a beauty pageant. Not the UK-based Miss World contest, mind you, but with its North American cousin: the US-based Miss Universe Organization.

My association with the pageant came through a friend, Miss Universe 2008 Dayana Mendoza. I met the stunning Venezuelan beauty when she and fellow Venezuelan—my friend and client, actress and model Patricia Velasquez—competed against each other in the 2012 season of *The Celebrity Apprentice*. They were joined by the likes of singers Clay Aiken and Aubrey O'Day together with talk show host Arsenio Hall, Bravo star Teresa Giudice, and supermodel Cheryl Tiegs.

After weeks of battling for survival, completing grueling tasks, and facing heated confrontations as well as Donald Trump in the boardroom, the experience had left the two women firm friends.

After the season wrapped, I stayed in touch with Dayana and she was the first person I thought of when Emin announced, in the spring of 2013, that he wanted to find "the most beautiful woman in the world" to co-star in the video for his new Latin-inspired song, "Amor." He didn't just want an actress or model but the world's most beautiful woman.

I told Dayana about the video and she loved the concept and seemed excited by the project, but wanted to hear more details. She put me in touch with her management to arrange logistics. I contacted them immediately, desperate to figure out how I could make the whole thing work. Dayana was unquestionably one of the most beautiful women I'd ever seen. In the end, however, she wasn't available, but she came up with a great idea. She offered to connect me with Paula Shugart, president of the Miss Universe Organization, who might be able to help me in the search for Emin's beautiful co-star.

I was thrilled at her suggestion. Not only would I be able to discuss the video project with Paula, but it would give me the opportunity to pitch Emin as a potential musical performer for a future Miss Universe telecast. If I could persuade her to book him, this would be a major coup since the contest has a worldwide television audience of over a billion viewers. That kind of exposure was the very thing needed to fast track Emin's singing career.

A few days after speaking with Dayana, I received a phone call from Paula while I was in a car headed to JFK airport. I was leaving for London and suggested we meet when I returned. I was delighted by her call, and remembered that Emin would also be in Manhattan at the same time, so suggested we all meet together.

Paula agreed that we should schedule to meet at the Miss Universe Organization's midtown offices, adding that a few of the women in her office had googled Emin and were swooning over his online pictures. They were eager to meet him and see if he lived up to the images in person.

I hung up with Paula and called Emin and told him about my conversation and the plan for us to meet with the Miss Universe team. Along with finding him a dazzling co-star, I explained my aim to lock him in as a performer on a future pageant telecast. He loved both ideas and agreed to the meeting at once.

A couple of weeks later, Emin and I were riding the elevator up to meet Paula on the sixteenth floor of the 56th Street building which housed the Miss Universe Organization offices. As the elevator doors opened, we were met by a hallway of bright pink walls and giant blowup photographs of Miss Universe, Miss USA, and Miss Teen USA. The current Miss Universe, Rhode Island-native Olivia Culpo, had been the reigning Miss USA before clinching the global title in 2012, thereby passing the Miss USA title to the runner-up: Nana Meriwether.

Emin and I took a few selfies in front of the photos of the title-holders and posted them at once on our social media. The receptionist appeared to recognize Emin and showed us directly into a conference room where we waited for Paula.

A few minutes later Paula joined us. A diminutive, no-nonsense straight-talker, she had an infectious laugh and playful sense of humor. Both Emin and I liked her immediately. She introduced us to four or five of her colleagues who were, she said, very keen to meet us. I gathered by "us," she meant Emin.

When the occasion called for it, Emin could charm anyone, and it didn't take long for them to be smitten by him. He made them laugh and told them crazy anecdotes (mostly about me). I told them all about his music career, including how he had been a special guest performer at the 2012 Eurovision Song Contest, which had been held in his birth country of Azerbaijan. At the mention of Azerbaijan, I noticed Paula look up and glance at her colleagues. She told us that only recently she had been discussing the possibility of staging the contest in the country's capital, Baku.

Emin and I looked at each other and smiled.

"I am not sure if you know this, but Emin was born in Baku and is that country's biggest star. He also happens to be married to the daughter of the president of Azerbaijan," I told a stunned Paula and her equally stunned team.

Before Paula had a chance to respond, Emin looked over at her and posed a question. In classic Emin style, it came out of nowhere: "Paula, have you ever thought about bringing the Miss Universe pageant to Russia?"

Paula looked a little surprised and said, "Well, yes. Many times actually," adding that all previous attempts to bring the pageant to Russia had ended in disappointment.

She said that these outreaches had proved unsuccessful, full of potential pitfalls, logistical difficulties, and endless red tape. She explained how only recently she had visited Moscow to attend the Miss Russia pageant and had toured a couple of potential venues suitable for staging a future Miss Universe pageant. She told us that she had been particularly impressed with one of the venues she had inspected: the newly opened Crocus City Hall.

Emin looked over to me and grinned. Then he nudged me, saying, "Rob, why don't you tell her?"

I looked at Paula and, with a straight face, asked, "What if you were able to do the deal directly with the owner of Crocus City Hall?"

Emin and his father's Crocus Group real estate empire owned and operated Crocus City Hall, and before Paula or any of her team had a chance to answer my question, Emin answered the question himself while simultaneously ramping it up to the next level with his trademark bullishness.

"Let's make this happen. We can definitely do it at Crocus City Hall, and I'll guarantee you that Moscow will be the best pageant you have ever had! Rob will handle the details and make it happen."

Can you really make a multimillion dollar decision on a complex international project in ten seconds with no discussion? Yes, if you're Emin. Can you leave the details of setting up such a monumental undertaking to your music manager? Again, yes, if you're Emin. And just like that, without warning, Emin stood up, thanked everyone for the meeting, and started to say his goodbyes to the Miss Universe team, who just sat there, speechless.

He assured Paula that the deal was as good as done. He added that I would be his liaison with the Miss Universe team, while his family's business associate Irakly "Ike" Kaveladze would work on all the financial and sponsorship aspects of the project, and would report directly to his father, Aras.

"You will definitely have your contest in Moscow later this year," Emin said as he reached the door to leave.

This is how I would witness Emin make many big decisions over the years: on impulse. Early on when we first began working together, he told me that no matter what the size of the numbers involved, the right decision is always the right decision. Conversely, he said, a bad decision is just as bad if it involves a few hundred dollars as it is if it involves a few million.

Emin was keen to leave and move on to our next appointment,

but I realized there was another issue we still needed to deal with. In all the excitement over the Agalarovs potentially staging the next Miss Universe pageant in Moscow, we had completely forgotten the reason we were there in the first place. We still needed Emin's co-star for his music video.

I asked everyone if they would sit back down again at the conference table while Emin played the "Amor" track a couple of times. Together, Emin and I tried to describe what we had in mind for the moody, sexy video that we were planning to shoot in Los Angeles in less than a month.

Although everyone seemed clearly preoccupied and stunned by Emin's pageant proposal a few minutes earlier, Paula and the team appeared to like the song and by the end of the meeting we had our beautiful co-star. It was none other than Miss Universe herself, Olivia Culpo. I couldn't imagine doing much better. Emin had asked me to find the most beautiful woman in the world, and we had done just that.

Eventually, Emin and I said our goodbyes to Paula and her team and got into the elevator. The meeting had been a great success and we were bubbling with excitement about what lay ahead. As we exited the building and headed to our next appointment, I realized the craziness of what had just happened and Emin's proposal: I would be helping to bring the Miss Universe pageant to Russia for the first time in the pageant's sixty-plus-year history.

Surely, this would surpass my mother's beauty contest story. I was certain that had she still been alive, she would have been *kvelling*.

Chapter Three

The Elvis of Azerbaijan

People ask me all the time how a British working-class boy from a council estate in Manchester ended up taking care of a billionaire pop star from Russia. The answer is simple: like so many things in my life, the opportunity to work with Emin came out of the blue and was thanks to an unexpected connection.

In 2012, I was handling publicity for a young singer-song-writer in New York whose manager was a close friend of Emin's then-manager. He asked me one afternoon if I would be interested in meeting with the Russian singer to discuss a publicity campaign to help launch him in the US. It seemed intriguing and, by a strange coincidence, I had spent six months as a teenager studying the Russian Cyrillic alphabet as a hobby, which I never thought would ever be of use to me.

I met Emin for the first time one afternoon in a Manhattan hotel, and within a few minutes we realized we shared the same outrageous sense of humor. From the very first meeting, we laughed at each other's jokes and took turns trying to out-shock each other with the most bizarre and outlandish comments and behavior we could come up with. Nothing was off limits.

On one memorable occasion in London, Emin became bored

during an afternoon of press interviews and decided to spice things up with a journalist from an Irish newspaper. When the writer asked him to share something people would be surprised to learn about him, he answered with a straight face that he liked to "eat human flesh." It took a moment for the journalist to realize that Emin was kidding around and not admitting to cannibalism.

During another interview he told a shocked reporter that his mother was a "heroin addict," and when that didn't get the desired reaction, he told the interviewer that I was a "sex machine." The writer looked at me, baffled, but nevertheless wrote a glowing piece on the charming if slightly off-the-wall Russian singer.

But Emin's all-time favorite prank took place whenever he was due to appear on live television. Moments before air-time, he would have me tell the interviewer that he didn't speak a word of English. As horror gripped the host, Emin would collapse into fits of giggles and I would be left to reassure the frazzled interviewer that Emin spoke perfect, if slightly accented, English. It never failed to send him into hysterics.

Emin Aras Oğlu Agalarov was born in Baku, Azerbaijan, on December 12, 1979, when the country was still part of the Soviet Union. The Agalarov family moved to Moscow when Emin was just four years old, and when he was thirteen his parents sent him to a private boarding school, the exclusive Institut Auf Dem Rosenberg in St. Gallen, Switzerland.

In 1995, the family moved from Moscow to the United States, making their home first in Tenafly, New Jersey, and later in nearby Alpine, one of the wealthiest zip codes in America. Emin once told me that the reason behind this sudden move was a horrifying incident in which the family's apartment building in Moscow had been firebombed. He said it was then that his father, one of Russia's new breed of rich businessmen, decided he had to get his family out of Moscow for their own safety.

During Emin's time at Tenafly High School, he met and formed lifelong friendships with two classmates: Jason Tropea and Roman Beniaminov. They would both stay close to him throughout his business and professional life. As well as being trusted pals and confidantes, to this day they work for him out of an office in New Jersey.

Emin easily adapted to his new life in America and, according to friends, was one of the most popular students in the school. As he got older, he became something of a playboy, driving fast cars, partying hard, and singing at open mic events in and around New Jersey. His love for music had begun with his maternal grandfather and also his mother Irina, who first introduced him to the music of Elvis Presley. As Emin got older, Presley became his idol.

Emin often told interviewers that he began singing and translating Elvis Presley's music as a way to practice his English, but soon he fell in love with the music itself. He mimicked Elvis's signature moves: the quivering lip, pelvic thrusts, and even some of the King's karate moves. To this day, Emin includes a medley of his favorite Elvis songs in most of his live concert performances. It would be a very proud and happy moment for Emin when he would read the headline of a feature, I had got him, in *The Wall Street Journal* which called him "The Elvis of Azerbaijan."

The other major musical influence in Emin's life and career was a close family friend, who was himself as famous as Elvis in the former Soviet Union. Muslim Magomayev has been called the greatest Soviet-era singing star of all time, and it was he who encouraged Emin's love of singing and championed his decision to pursue music professionally—much to Aras's initial dismay. Emin was his only son and heir to the billion dollar Crocus business empire that Aras had built from nothing. To him, Emin's singing was nothing more than a hobby. Years later, at Emin's debut concert, Aras was asked by a TV interviewer what he thought of his son's performance. He answered candidly that he wasn't a fan.

Emin ultimately succeeded in winning his father over, and Aras would go on to attend almost all of Emin's concerts, sitting front and center, beaming with pride and applauding as if he was Emin's number one fan.

No sooner had Emin met me in New York, then he hired me and my company, Oui 2 Public Relations, to handle his US publicity. I didn't know exactly how I was going to get PR for an unknown Russian singer in America, but I was willing to use every trick in my book to make it happen. No Russian pop singer had ever crossed over into mainstream Western music. There had been a couple of successful attempts by novelty acts such as the girl group t.A.T.u., but no singer-songwriter had ever made it here.

Emin had already experienced some international success with a couple of his singles chosen as *Record of the Week* by BBC Radio 2, the UK's leading music station. That was a meaningful and impressive accomplishment since the UK is one of the hardest music markets in the world to crack.

He had also performed as guest artist at the Eurovision Song Contest which had helped make his name in Europe. While most Americans may have never heard of Eurovision, it is, in fact, the largest international singing contest in the world with an estimated audience of over two hundred million TV viewers.

One reason I was confident that I could get Emin media attention in the States was his background. This was not just an average Russian singer looking for a US audience. Emin was a mini-oligarch in his own right, controlling a multimillion, perhaps even billion dollar real estate and luxury lifestyle empire, comprising dozens of restaurants, major fashion brands, entertainment venues, and luxury shopping malls.

The idea of a billionaire pop star with Ricky Martin looks and

Michael Bublé charm was something I thought people would be interested in. The UK press had already nicknamed Emin the "Russian Ricky Martin" and *British Esquire* had dubbed him "Michael Bubléiski."

Once I was officially hired as Emin's publicist, I began to put my ideas into action and soon had him performing and being interviewed on local and national TV shows in the US and the UK, where he never failed to charm the hosts.

Emin's official US launch was a great success, and I got him signed to a worldwide music publishing contract with Sony ATV, the world's largest music publisher, and a distribution deal with a division of Warner Music Group. We were making incredible progress, and my PR and marketing plan was working better than anticipated. Emin was happy and energized and keen to take his music career to the next level.

Still, there were some initial issues I had to address when I first began working with him. The biggest one was his misunderstanding that he was already making inroads into the US music market. In interviews and in conversation, he would mention his music charting in *Billboard* magazine. Being an avid reader of the industry bible, that was certainly news to me. After repeating the claim yet again, I took him aside and addressed the subject head on.

"Are you crazy? You're not on any official *Billboard* chart," I said.

He looked momentarily shocked before calmly assuring me, as you might someone who is misinformed, that he was, in fact, on the chart.

"Have you ever seen your name in the magazine, in this chart?" I said.

Emin explained that he'd been told there was no physical magazine, just an online chart, so there wasn't a magazine to look in.

"No," I said. "There is a magazine." And to make my point, I decided the best way was to show him the reality.

A few days later I took Emin to the *Billboard* offices and introduced him to the magazine's publisher and some of the writing and chart staff I'd come to know over the years. They told him what I had told him, that he definitely had not charted on any *Billboard* chart. It turned out Emin had "charted" on some kind of pay-for-play digital chart, which he had been assured was the same thing. It wasn't.

This episode proved a turning point in our relationship and his level of trust in me. For years he would retell this story to friends and colleagues, emphasizing that I had never once told him that something was wrong, but, instead, had shown him.

Six months later, he asked me to be his manager. I was flattered, but declined. I ran a boutique PR company, which meant I had a hands-on approach with each and every one of my clients. I knew taking on Emin as his personal manager would be something wholly different and be a 24/7 job. It would mean I'd have to give up my business and concentrate solely on him—a daunting prospect. It seemed just too risky to put all my eggs into one basket, and it was for that reason, more than any other, that I declined his offer. To my astonishment, Emin simply ignored my rejection. He asked me again. I declined again. And then he asked again.

But I stood my ground, and was still resolute in my decision the first time I visited him in Moscow. Emin, on the other hand, had other ideas. By the time my flight from New York landed at Moscow's Sheremetyevo Airport, Emin had begun to put the pieces in place for me to be his manager, and had already wired the first month's management fee into my bank account. It was one of the few times in my life I was truly speechless.

I reminded him that I had said "no" to being his manager, but his response was classic Emin.

"You can call yourself whatever you want. I will simply call you my manager."

I realized then and there that Emin had a way of getting what he wanted. Time and again throughout the coming years of our working together, I would be reminded of this fact.

Upon landing, I was assigned my own driver and de-facto bodyguard, a former police officer named Sasha, who I immediately nicknamed "Sushi." Nothing was ever too much trouble for him and, it seemed, he was on call for me twenty-four hours a day. Whatever time it was, Sushi was outside, waiting, ready to get me through a snowstorm or the endless Moscow traffic jams to wherever I needed to go.

Sushi worked for Emin's head of security, Andrei Valeryevich, an eagle-eyed, perfectly groomed character who had the posture of an army sergeant and reminded me of someone from a James Bond movie. He was never more than a few steps away from Emin, his eyes constantly scanning the crowd, his face expressionless and intimidating. Although he was never anything but polite to me, all it took was his subtle nod and not-so-subtle handshake to leave me in no doubt that he was a truly terrifying human being.

I was staying at the Ritz Carlton Hotel, steps from Red Square, and I spent my first full day in Moscow exploring Crocus City. This was Emin and Aras's pride and joy, a sprawling shopping and leisure complex that was a small city unto itself. It even had its own subway station, recently built, of course, by Aras, to maximize visitors.

The development is anchored by Crocus City Mall, one of the most luxurious shopping complexes I've ever seen. An enormous space of cream marble and neoclassical architecture with lush foliage and pools featuring synchronized swimmers, the mall houses some of the most sought after designer names in the world, including Prada, Chanel, Vivienne Westwood, John Varvatos, Loro Piana, Max Mara, Ermenegildo Zegna, Lanvin, Sergio Rossi, Escada, Kenzo, among dozens of others. Crocus City Mall is a serene haven for Moscow's rich and elite.

But arguably the crowning glory of the Crocus City development is Crocus City Hall. The impressive, newly built concert hall was impeccably designed, featured state-of-the-art acoustics, and, most importantly for me, had seventy-five hundred extremely comfortable large red plush seats. Paula had been right when she said during our first meeting that this would be the perfect venue to stage the Miss Universe pageant.

During that first visit to Moscow, Emin's charm was on overdrive as he introduced me to his beloved city, a city where if you had money and influence, you could easily believe you were in London, Paris, or Beverly Hills. Opulent apartment buildings, luxury stores, and impeccable restaurants lined grand boulevards and tree-filled squares.

Moscow was a place I had wanted to visit ever since I was a teenager studying the Russian alphabet. In those days, the Soviet Union was a mysterious, almost mythical place, where few tourists were able or permitted to journey to and discover it for themselves.

Now, all these years later, I was there, in the heart of Moscow. And as I stood with Emin in Red Square, at the end of my first day in Russia, taking a cellphone photo in front of the iconic onion-domed St. Basil's Cathedral, the giant clock behind us struck midnight.

I knew that this was the beginning of a new chapter in my life.

Chapter Four

To Russia with Love

Paula and her team, including the reigning Miss Universe Olivia Culpo, arrived in Moscow a few days after me. They were on a scouting trip to identify sites, hotels, transportation, and production and broadcast facilities for the upcoming pageant.

But most importantly, they were also hoping to get a signed contract from Emin's father Aras, since the deadline for announcing the location of the contest was fast approaching. It was of paramount importance that the Agalarovs and the Miss Universe Organization reached agreement on all the key factors quickly.

Even though I believed we had identified all the major issues well in advance, there turned out to be a few important sticking points, including one that threatened to derail the entire telecast. Due to Moscow's seven-hour time difference, Paula said the contest needed to start at around 3 a.m. at Crocus City Hall in order to fit into NBC's traditional primetime evening broadcast in the United States.

When I approached Emin with this news, he told me he would never agree to the show taking place in the middle of the night. He was adamant, stating that they could not expect an audience at that hour. He added that it would also scupper their plans for a star-studded gala event and exclusive VIP after party.

He told me there would be no pageant unless I persuaded Paula to pre-tape the show at around 9 p.m. Moscow time, and then have NBC broadcast it, as if live, to the American audience the following day. It would not be an easy sell. I knew that a delayed broadcast would mean the winner would already be known well before the official TV show aired in the US. Not only did I think Paula might refuse to tape delay the show, but I imagined NBC would put up a huge fight as well.

I would need to pick just the right moment to broach this issue with Paula, but I decided that first I needed to make sure the contest was actually going to get the green light in Moscow. Without Aras signing a contract in the next few days, it seemed pointless to think about any of the potential conflicts.

For one thing, there had to be some agreement on the total cost of the undertaking. A host city or venue was required to provide not just a cash fee for the rights to stage the contest, which in this case was six million dollars, but also many more millions of dollars in goods and services. This included hundreds of hotel rooms, meals, ground transportation, and international and domestic air travel for the pageant staff, judges, performers, and VIPs. It could add up to nine million dollars or more. That meant the Agalarovs would be committing to underwrite up to fifteen million dollars.

That kind of multimillion dollar commitment needed to be carefully weighed against the international exposure and enormous publicity value that this kind of event would generate.

I knew that ultimately the world's media would descend on Crocus City Hall and Emin would be front and center, not just as a charming host in Moscow, but also as an international musical performer. He would be seen by an estimated one billion TV viewers, and would take the stage along with other world-class performers including Panic! At The Disco and the legendary

Steven Tyler of Aerosmith. This was my major focus. I believed it could open doors around the globe for Emin and help with our soon-to-be-released international CD.

After a week of site visits and endless meetings, I still didn't know for sure if Moscow would be the location of the 2013 contest. That decision would ultimately rest with Aras. I did know, however, that time was running out.

On Paula and her team's last night in Moscow, Emin organized a farewell dinner for them. So keen were Paula's team to lock in Moscow for November's contest, they brought with them both a draft contract and a letter of intent for Aras to sign. Paula confided in me as we sat down for dinner that she couldn't get a read on Aras, and wasn't sure if they would leave Moscow with his signature on either of the documents. She told me that realistically, if he didn't sign at least the letter of intent at this dinner, there was little chance of the contest coming to Moscow because of the time constraints, and most likely it would be staged once again in Las Vegas.

The farewell dinner was being held at Zafferano, my favorite of all of Emin's twenty-plus restaurants, which sat atop the elegant Lotte Hotel in Moscow's city center. It was casual but chic and had a spacious outdoor terrace overlooking uber-cool Arbat Street. It reminded me of the trendy bistros you find in Los Angeles, but the food was authentic Azerbaijani cuisine, which I would grow to love as I spent time around Emin and his family and friends both in Moscow and Baku. Two of my favorite dishes there were *saj* which reminded me of an old fashioned British beef stew, and *jiz-biz* which I loved as much for its name as how it tasted. That night I ordered both.

There were more than twenty people seated at one long table, including Paula and her team, Olivia Culpo, Emin, some of his close friends, and the man everyone was focused on: Aras.

Although on paper there was the potential to recoup much of the multimillion dollar investment through ticket sales, broadcast rights, and sponsorship and partner opportunities, without a guarantee of government support and/or a major outside sponsor of the project, all the burden of financial responsibility would fall on Aras.

If this event failed, I would feel that it was partly my fault, since I had been the one who made the initial introduction between the Agalarovs and the Miss Universe team. I thought the chances of the deal happening were 50/50 at best. Given that my job was Emin's music manager, it was a pretty big stretch to see how I had suddenly become the pivotal middleman to help pull off this ginormous event.

We were about to begin the sixth or seventh round of traditional Russian vodka shot toasts, something all visitors to Russia learn is a way of life there. I, however, had perfected the art of using water to fill my shot glass when no one was looking, because I don't drink vodka.

Emin pulled me to one side and out of the blue whispered, "Go speak with my father and see if you can get him to make a decision right now, sign the letter, and say yes to the contest. It would be amazing to end the dinner tonight with the announcement and a celebration."

"I can't just go up to your father and convince him to go ahead with a fifteen-million-dollar deal," I replied, adding that apart from anything else, Aras barely spoke or understood English.

Then Emin repeated the mantra he had told me so many times before: "Forget the size of the number. A good deal is a good deal. Take off the zeros if it makes it easier for you, Rob. Pretend it's a fifteen thousand dollar deal, not a fifteen-million-dollar one," he said.

The size of the potential investment was terrifying to me. I didn't operate in this world of endless zeros. My forte was dealing with large egos, not large investments. How was I now being asked to advise a billionaire on a decision involving millions of dollars for a deal that had come about on a whim? After all, our initial meeting with the Miss Universe team had been about finding a co-star for a music video and trying to get Emin booked to perform on the show.

It was obvious to me that Emin and Aras saw the upside in having the contest in their venue in Moscow. Not only would it showcase their Crocus City properties to the world, but it would also showcase Emin as a world-class pop star.

There was another major upside no one had addressed as yet, but which I believed held massive potential future opportunities for the Agalarovs. That was Donald Trump.

As co-owner of the Miss Universe pageant, which he had purchased in 1996, Trump would be front and center of this project and would be a partner in the Moscow contest with the Agalarovs, who themselves had been dubbed the "Trumps of Russia." Like Trump, the Agalarovs had built a real estate empire and, like Trump, they had diversified into entertainment.

But unlike Trump, Aras Agalarov had come from humble beginnings. He started building his multimillion dollar empire in the last days of the Soviet Union. He was completely self-made, and vehemently proud of it. Emin told me how his father had once earned money by copying popular Western movies onto video and selling them on the black market. From there, he went on to dabble in the fast-growing computer market in Russia; and when the Soviet Union collapsed in 1989, he saw a huge opportunity in creating an expo business in Russia.

Aras went from one success to another, and soon became the owner of the largest expo and convention halls in Moscow. At the same time, he began to buy up pieces of land in a disused suburb on the outskirts of the city. That land would eventually be developed by him and his son to create Crocus City, its own self-contained metropolis.

As I walked over to Aras to have the fifteen-million-dollar chat, it occurred to me that a Trump Tower Moscow probably wouldn't be far off if all went well. I approached Aras at the bar where he was chatting with some friends and waited for the right moment. Then I asked him in very simple language what his thoughts were on bringing the pageant to Moscow in November.

Paula and one of her team had positioned themselves directly opposite me at the other end of the bar. She later told me that she was trying to read my lips and judge Aras's body language. She said she was certain that I was having "the conversation."

Aras nodded a lot, smiled broadly, and said just three words to me, "It's good, no?"

At once I understood what he was asking. He appeared to want me to reassure him that he should spend fifteen million dollars to bring Miss Universe to Moscow.

I took a deep breath, remembered Emin's mantra, and replied, "It's good, yes!"

He shook my hand as if to seal the deal, and out of the corner of my eye I saw Paula break into the biggest smile I had seen during her entire week in Moscow. At that moment, Miss Universe was destined to come to Moscow in just a few months' time.

It was left for me to reveal the good news to Emin, who then called for yet another vodka toast to celebrate. It was one of the rare occasions that I deemed it worthy of replacing water in my shot glass with actual vodka, and joined Emin in chanting the Russian toast…*Na Zdorovie!*

Chapter Five

What Happens in Vegas...

It was mid-June, a few weeks after I had met with the Miss Universe delegation in Moscow, when I flew to Las Vegas for the Miss USA pageant. I was heading there in two capacities. First, Paula had invited me to be a preliminary judge. She figured that with my background in journalism, I would be a helpful addition to the team that was tasked with interviewing the fifty-one contestants in order to narrow them down to the final fifteen.

Contrary to popular belief, the winner of the pageant was expected to be as smart and confident as she was beautiful. Paula had put together a team of prelim judges from a variety of backgrounds and fields who she hoped would bring their unique perspectives to the judging process.

When Paula had mentioned, in Moscow, the idea of being a pageant judge, I jumped at the possibility. Maybe a little too enthusiastically. Apart from being a once-in-a-lifetime experience, I thought it would give me insight into what went into creating and staging the event. This should prove invaluable, later in November, when the Miss Universe pageant would come to Moscow.

The second reason I was headed to Las Vegas was significantly more important than the first. I was there to meet with Emin and his family to help orchestrate the first encounter between the Agaralovs and Donald Trump. I knew that it was important for the pageant that Emin and Aras establish a rapport with Trump during their time together in Vegas. But before I could begin worrying about that meeting, I had to concentrate on selecting my fifteen finalists.

The work of a prelim judge is very different from that of the celebrity judges who choose the eventual winner, live on television, at the climax of the pageant. Celebrity judges make their decision from a group of fifteen, chosen by prelim judges like me.

Upon arrival in Vegas, we were given binders containing the names, statistics, resumes, and photographs of each of the contestants vying to be Miss USA 2013. We were advised to study the information carefully, and use it as the basis of our questioning during the interviews to follow.

During the lunch break, one of my fellow judges told me how every year someone asks the reigning Miss Louisiana the same cheeky question which, he said, always got a laugh. It surprised no one, including myself, when I was the one chosen to deliver the playfully provocative question. A few minutes later, when we returned to the interview room, I confidently asked:

"Miss Louisiana, do you like to suck the head?"

Now to those in the know, it was obvious I was referring to Louisiana's popular saying about "pinching the tail then sucking the head" of a crawfish. But having just delivered the line, I prayed that she was a fan of shellfish as well as Louisiana popular culture. Everyone around me burst out laughing, including a smiling Miss Louisiana, who thankfully was familiar with that saying, and told me that indeed it was her favorite way to eat them.

I decided it was too good an opportunity to use just on the one contestant, and so, out of the blue, I asked the same question to the next contestant. My fellow judges thought it even more hilarious, but one sharp glance from Paula convinced me to move on, swiftly, to another line of questioning.

The following day was the prelim finals and the day we were to cast our votes live in front of cheering fans. The biggest issue for me was deciding what I could wear that would make me look about fifty pounds lighter on the giant screens all around the venue.

We all took our seats like *American Idol* judges directly in front of the stage and two hours later I had made my final decisions and my job was complete.

Part one of my Vegas adventure was now over, but the next, bigger part, still lay ahead of me. Aras, Emin, his mother Irina, sister Sheila, and some of their close friends were scheduled to arrive in Vegas the day before the pageant final. They were flying in on Aras's Gulfstream 550 jet, a super-sleek luxury aircraft which could accommodate up to nineteen guests. The aircraft boasted a fully operational kitchen, deluxe bathroom, and plush leather seats worthy of any five-star hotel. I had been a pampered passenger on this plane on a few occasions, and it certainly took flying to a whole new level of comfort and extravagance.

Aras was coming to Vegas not just to meet with Donald Trump, but to sign the all-important contract with the Miss Universe Organization, so that Trump could make the official Moscow announcement on stage, at a press conference, after the crowning of the new Miss USA. Although Aras had already signed a letter of intent back in Moscow, the official contract was still to be signed by him, and would be completed only a few hours before the scheduled announcement.

On the morning of their arrival, I went straight to the Trump International Hotel. While we were all given suites, Aras was given the most jaw-dropping VIP suite I had ever seen, spacious enough to host a hundred people or more comfortably in its living room alone.

As luck would have it, no sooner had I spotted the Agalarov party walking into the hotel, I also spotted Donald Trump at the opposite end of the lobby, signing autographs and taking pictures with a group of fans. Suddenly, Trump bellowed across the foyer, "Look who has come to see me! The richest man in Russia and his family." He gestured to Aras and Emin to come over and join him. Aras seemed a little embarrassed as Emin translated what Trump had said, not least, perhaps, because Aras didn't even make the top fifty of Russia's richest oligarchs according to Forbes magazine. Aras was many tens of billions of dollars away from occupying the number one position.

As they shook hands, Trump said to Aras, "You are a great family with a wonderful business. I know that's true, because I had you checked out." *Only half-joking or maybe not joking at all,* I thought. Trump complimented Aras and Emin on their Crocus City development and said he looked forward to visiting the giant complex during the pageant in Moscow in November.

Emin then introduced me as his music manager, telling Trump that I was working with Paula and her team to make sure the pageant was the most "amazing" ever. Emin had started to share much of Trump's characteristic hyperbole, and it was on full display at this first meeting.

As an icebreaker, I reminded Donald Trump that I had met him already on a number of occasions, most recently when he "walked" one of our red carpets in NYC, at a gala honoring broadcaster Larry King. I reminded him that I had represented actress Patricia Velasquez who had competed in The Celebrity Apprentice the previous year. He nodded politely, but clearly he had no recollection of either occasion.

Trump said he would have to excuse himself because he was headed to a rehearsal to meet the contestants, who were due on stage shortly. He invited us to join him there after we checked in.

We took him up on his offer, taking Ike Kaveladze with us. Ike was the Agalarovs' trusted business associate and would work alongside me on various financial aspects of the upcoming pageant, reporting directly to Emin and Aras. Coincidentally, he would also be the person tasked with coordinating the Trump Tower meeting in June 2016, and would attend along with the Russian delegation.

Trump was shadowed by a tall, serious-looking man, Keith Schiller, who he introduced as his personal head of security. Emin shook his hand and explained to Keith that the Agalarovs' own head of security would be his direct liaison in Moscow in November during Trump's visit. If it was one thing the Agalarovs did well, it was security.

They had a team of highly trained bodyguards and drivers around the clock ensuring the safety of themselves and their guests. I had witnessed many times the impressive driving skills of the Agalarov security team, mostly while being driven at breakneck speed in formation around the streets and highways of Moscow. One of the drivers told me how they had been trained to keep a one-car distance behind the leader at all times by having a piece of rope attached to the bumpers of each vehicle and completing a journey without the rope snapping. It may sound simple, but in reality it's extraordinarily difficult.

As we were leaving the rehearsal, Emin told me he had organized dinner at Wolfgang Puck's restaurant CUT at the Palazzo Hotel. He said it would be a casual meal for just his family, me, and some of his friends who were also in Vegas.

I was back in my room, changing for dinner, when the hotel phone rang. Keith Schiller was on the other end.

"Hey Rob, Mr. Trump heard you guys were going to dinner tonight and would like to join you. Is that okay?" he asked.

Momentarily surprised, I told him it would be our pleasure. It seemed I was now responsible for Donald Trump having a good time as well as the Agalarovs. I called Emin to give him the news.

"You must have made a good impression," I said. "He wants to come to dinner with us."

"Who does?" asked Emin.

"Trump! His security guy just called."

"You're joking, right?" Emin said with a nervous laugh.

"I'll leave it with you to make it work," said Emin. "And make sure you sit next to me and Trump."

I suddenly realized I hadn't asked Schiller if Trump was coming alone or bringing guests. I would now need to create some kind of seating chart, expand the table size, and dinner was in forty-five minutes.

My next call was to Paula. I found her in the middle of last minute rehearsals, but was convinced I should tell her that her boss was unexpectedly coming to dinner.

"You can't be serious?" she said, sounding a little horrified.

I knew tonight was the busiest part of the week and included a full dress rehearsal, so her shock was understandable. Paula was silent for a few seconds before telling me that she would also now be coming to dinner, and for good measure, would be bringing Olivia Culpo. Paula also suggested I should plan on having a spare seat or two just in case Trump invited friends.

"Absolutely. Not a problem," I lied.

Next I called the restaurant to beg them to increase the size of our already cramped dinner table. The restaurant was packed to capacity and reluctant to make last minute changes, but after dropping the name Donald Trump a dozen or so times, I convinced them to put us in a private room and expand the table to accommodate our unspecified number of guests.

I arrived a few minutes before everyone else to check the room and work out a seating plan. Emin arrived a few minutes later and decided he would sit at the center of the table with Trump on one side of him and me on the other. Aras would sit directly opposite Trump so Emin could act as translator.

Years later, during the RussiaGate scandal, cellphone footage of this dinner would be shopped to the media and sold to CNN by a guest who had attended the dinner. The footage was shown around the world to illustrate the apparent closeness of Donald Trump to the Agalarovs, and to me. In reality, we had known Trump, at that point, for about three hours.

Trump arrived right on time with Schiller and another guest, who introduced himself as Trump's friend and attorney, Michael Cohen. I found myself with Emin on one side and Cohen on my other. Trump sat between Emin and Olivia. Cocktails and champagne had been served to all except Trump, who, we were told, never drank alcohol, preferring Diet Coke. As dinner began, I could see that he and Emin were chatting away and appeared to be hitting it off.

Trump and Michael Cohen each spoke of previous attempts to take the pageant to Russia, but both said they could never find a partner they could trust and so plans had always hit a roadblock. Cohen repeated Trump's earlier claim about "checking out" the Agalarovs, adding that this time they believed they had found partners they could trust and do business with in order to make the pageant a success.

One of my aims during dinner was to ensure that Trump agreed to spend at least two full days in Moscow during the pageant. The Agalarovs wanted to organize a series of high-level promotional activities for him, and needed reassurance that he would be there and on board.

One important event on the list was an exclusive cocktail reception where Trump would be the guest of honor and address a gathering of some of Russia's most influential banking and business leaders. This powerhouse soirée was scheduled for the day before the pageant and would be held at Nobu Moscow, a restaurant co-owned by Emin along with actor Robert De Niro, Chef Nobu Matsuhisa, and businessman Meir Tapper.

The event would be a chance for the Agalarovs to show off their special VIP guest to their peers, who, I had been told, were all intrigued and excited at the prospect of meeting Trump.

The other event I needed him to agree to attend was arguably even more important. Directly following the Nobu reception, there would be a huge party in honor of Aras's fifty-eighth birthday. Emin would host the celebrity-filled gala for hundreds of important guests, and my job was to ensure that the number one most important attendee, Donald Trump, was front and center of this spectacular celebration.

As the Vegas dinner progressed, I leaned behind Emin and asked Trump how much time he would be spending in Moscow. I told him about the two important events that were now already on the calendar, and added that there were also a number of high profile media activities for him to attend with hundreds of journalists expected to cover the pageant.

This innocuous gesture, in which I leaned behind Emin to ask Donald Trump these few scheduling questions, would be later used by the media as "evidence" of my close friendship with Trump.

Trying to play all my *Trump* cards at dinner, I told him how Russia loved him, and that the anticipated reaction to his arrival in Moscow would be overwhelming. I had witnessed many Russians in awe of Trump, not just for his business skills, but for his praise and admiration for President Putin. This was happening at a time when most of the world appeared to be firmly against the Russian leader.

Trump nodded in agreement to everything I was saying, but I

wasn't sure if he was actually agreeing to my requests, or just trying to get me to shut up. Either way, I took it to mean yes.

Then, out of nowhere, Trump leaned over to Emin and with a mischievous smile said loudly: "I'll reduce the fee for the pageant by a million dollars if you tell me right now if you've slept with any of the contestants."

There was a pause. Trump was smiling.

Emin, not to be outdone by Trump's provocative question, smiled and with his eyes twinkling, said: "Mr. Trump, I will add five million dollars to the fee if you tell me right now if you've ever slept with any contestants."

Trump smiled again. It was obvious that he appreciated the fact that Emin could give as good as he got.

"Interesting," said Trump. "Why don't we just forget the bet?"

I knew right then and there this was a match made in frat boy heaven. I remember thinking that I had made a great hook up with these two, and surely it could only be good for Emin's music career, let alone any future business ideas they might conjure up.

Later that evening, Trump showed a self-deprecating side that is rarely seen these days. During a conversation between him and Emin's mother Irina, Trump asked how she was traveling back from Vegas to her home in New Jersey and offered her a seat on his plane if she needed one.

Irina politely declined, saying she would be flying with her husband and family on Aras's jet. Trump seemed intrigued and asked Aras about his plane.

The modest oligarch told him, with Emin translating, that although he currently owned a Gulfstream 550, he was in fact scheduled to receive one of the highly coveted new Gulfstream 650 jets, a fact that seemed to excite Trump, who suddenly exclaimed loudly to Irina: "That's the difference between your husband and me. I would have told everyone right away that I was one of only a few people on earth able to secure that particular jet. Yet Aras didn't even mention owning a plane, let alone this one, until I asked him about it."

Adding my two cents to the mix, I couldn't help telling Irina that maybe she should accept Trump's offer of the flight and perhaps one day, who knows, she could be a future wife of the real estate billionaire.

"Been there, done that, not interested," she replied in a perfect deadpan delivery to roars of laughter from everyone at the table.

Dinner was finally coming to an end, and one of our guests invited us to join him and his friends at the sexy Vegas nightclub, The Act. The club, I was told, was a tamer version of its world-renowned sister club, The Box, which had a reputation for erotic, provocative, artistic, and acrobatic performances in its always-packed New York and London locations.

It therefore came as something of a shock when Keith whispered to me that Trump wanted to come with us. I somehow didn't picture Donald Trump in a packed Vegas nightclub with what I imagined would be a sexy burlesque version of Cirque du Soleil.

"He must like you guys; he never stays this long at a dinner, and now he wants to go with you to the club," said Keith.

Thirty minutes later we all squeezed into a tiny VIP area in one of the most packed clubs I had ever been in, and made small talk as performers did their "act" all around us. It was sexy, sultry, and indeed provocative. It was later written that some of the performers on stage simulated urinating onto the crowd as part of their performance. But no one did that particular "act" at The Act that night, at least, to the best of my recollection.

At the club, Trump appeared to be having a great time and showed no signs of wanting to leave. Emin couldn't resist making his usual series of jokes about me being a "sex machine," and made everyone laugh as he proceeded to pinch, bite, and try to scare me by jumping out from under a nearby table. I knew this routine was Emin's way of putting people at ease when first meeting them; and to Emin, Trump was no different from anyone else he wanted to charm and make feel comfortable.

As the night wore on, we could barely hide our exhaustion, but knew we couldn't leave until our VIP guest was ready to go. Emin kept whispering to me, asking when Trump might eventually leave, but it appeared that there was no end in sight. It was close to 2 a.m. when Trump finally said goodnight, and we could all return to the hotel.

"You are good guys," he said as he shook our hands.

It seemed obvious to me that the evening had been a success, and I went to sleep believing that he would say yes to all my Moscow requests. Once again, it appeared I was going to make the impossible possible.

Chapter Six

Delicate Child

As a baby born into Manchester's close-knit Jewish community, it was strange that I would end up being named after a Roman Catholic nun. In fact, it came as a total surprise to everyone, including my father, who, on the day I was born, still believed my name was Russell. Only when the maternity nurse told him there was no baby named Russell born that day did he find out the truth: that immediately following my birth, exhausted and grateful, my mother had decided to name me after Sister Roberta, the nun who had stayed with her the entire time and assisted in my difficult delivery.

My parents, Bertha and Ike, had me late in life after having given up hope of ever having a child. When I finally did arrive, they couldn't help but overindulge me. I was what they called a "contrary" baby: one who slept all day and cried all night. For my already exhausted working parents, the burden of this schedule frazzled every last nerve. While there were plenty of unmarried older aunts in the family to care for me during the day, it was still tough on my parents.

Years later, my mother admitted that she had, out of desperation, resorted to giving me sugary Carnation evaporated milk in my bottle to comfort me and stop the endless nightly crying. Evaporated milk would later change to chocolate bars when infant crying turned into toddler temper tantrums. Unsurprisingly, I turned from a bouncing baby into an even bouncier toddler, my weight ballooning to more than one hundred-fifty pounds by the time I was eight.

Eventually, my mother had to come to terms with the fact that my weight was a health concern, and she realized that I needed to see a specialist doctor. During the examination, I heard a lot of words I didn't understand—glandular and endocrine, among others. After the examination was over, we were called into the doctor's office and I still remember the words he addressed to my mother.

"Unless this child is taken into a hospital immediately to lose weight, there's a very strong chance he could die within six months."

I thought she was going to cry, and I had never seen my mother cry. He told her that he would research some options and someone would contact us in a few days. I knew the situation was serious by my mother's reaction, but had no idea what lay ahead. I was rewarded later that day for having behaved well, ironically, with a chocolate bar.

The subject of going into hospital was never mentioned in front of me again, but a few weeks later my mum told me that I would be going to a boarding school with the improbable name of Delamere Forest School (for Delicate Jewish Children). Delicate seemed an odd way to describe me, but it didn't matter, because I was determined not to go.

One morning, not long after, there was a knock at the door of our first-floor flat, and the oldest looking woman I'd ever seen was standing on the doorstep. She had a gaunt pointed face with thinning silvery hair pulled tightly back. She was dressed in a severe looking gray woolen suit. She said her name was Margaret

Langdon, and I would later learn that she was the revered founder of Delamere Forest School.

It appeared that such was my importance to her school, that she had come to collect me herself. Miss Langdon and my parents had apparently discussed this, and they explained to me that I would be going there for three months. She bent down and whispered that the school was located in a wonderful place next to a magnificent forest in the Cheshire countryside, and that I would make lots of new friends there, and there'd be people around to help me lose weight.

There is no accurate way to fully describe the ensuing tantrum I threw, the likes of which I am sure even the revered Miss Langdon had never witnessed. But no matter how much I kicked and screamed, it seemed that the decision had already been made. There was no going back.

As I left my house, I shouted loudly to my parents that I hated them and that they would likely never see me again. They were clearly upset, but had to let me go, and so I kept my protest going as I got into the waiting car. I refused to speak a single word to Miss Langdon for the entire ninety-minute ride.

Margaret Langdon was a prominent Jewish philanthropist who had founded Delamere Forest School in 1921 for "delicate" Jewish children. Many of these children had special physical, emotional, and educational needs.

We finally arrived at the school, and I timidly got out of the car clutching my favorite teddy bear named Aloysius. I was walked across the playground by Miss Langdon and introduced to the school headmaster, Bernard Benjamin. He shook my hand, welcomed me to Delamere, and informed me that it was almost bedtime. I didn't understand what he meant. How could it be bedtime? It was barely four o'clock in the afternoon.

Miss Langdon saw my puzzled expression and told me that the

school operated on a fresh air principle of rising each day around dawn, going for long walks in the neighboring forest before breakfast, and after a full day of lessons and outdoor exercise, pupils would be in bed each day by four-thirty in the afternoon, with lights out by six. I was horrified. My parents had never cared what time I woke up or went to bed, for that matter. I was my own timekeeper at home, and I was determined to keep it that way here.

It wasn't long before I realized that my parents and Miss Langdon had lied to me about how long I would be at Delamere. Three months soon elapsed and there was no sign of my impending departure. While I was steadily losing weight, as a result of what I considered starvation tactics, I wanted out. If they couldn't give me my departure date, I would create my own.

Each morning as we did our daily exercises and took brisk walks through Delamere Forest, I plotted an escape route. I knew that if I could hide out in the woods for a day or so, I could get to a main road, flag down a car and beg the driver to take me back home, and make my shocking entrance.

I had begun to whisper my idea into the ears of some of the other kids and they told me that they also wanted to join my escape group. As the ringleader, the details and plans were left to me, and I decided that the best escape would be at night which, in theory, would give us at least six hours before anyone would discover we were missing.

Our group spent the next couple of weeks planning every detail of the grand escape down to the exact route we would take deep into the forest, the spot where we would make camp for the night, and the exit point near the all-important busy main road.

The night of our escape was less than forty-eight hours away when we were all summoned into the assembly hall by the headmaster. The staff looked solemn and I was sure that my plans must have been discovered. I could not imagine what lay ahead for me.

The headmaster got up onto the main stage and said he had been told some very disturbing information which he needed to share with us all.

"What I am about to tell you is very serious, and involves Delamere Forest, so I want you all to listen carefully," said Mr. Benjamin, looking more grim-faced than I had ever seen him look before.

I felt sick and knew that my escape plot was about to be unveiled to the entire school. I felt like I was about to throw up.

The headmaster continued: "The police have just informed me that last night in Delamere Forest, not far from our school, two French campers were murdered."

Everyone gasped. I, however, had never been so relieved in my entire life. I wanted to stand up and cheer with joy. My plans had not been discovered, and we could still leave the next day!

"For the time being, we are all banned from going into the forest, while the police hunt for the killers," said a still solemn Mr. Benjamin.

Despite the relief of knowing that my secret was safe, it dawned on me that I'd had a close call. What if I had led this escape forty-eight hours earlier? Would my friends and I now be dead? We could easily have been the target of the murderer and not those two French campers. At that moment, I abandoned my plan to escape.

I went on to spend not three months, but almost four years at Delamere, losing almost half my body weight, and becoming one of the most argumentative, annoying, and disruptive students in the school's history.

In many ways, I'm grateful for my time at Delamere because, if nothing else, it helped instill in me a survival instinct that would get me through life. That was something I would need in my next school, which was neither delicate nor Jewish.

At thirteen, I began attending Heys Boys' School, a rough and tumble secondary modern in Manchester, which was unlike anything I'd ever known. On day one, I found myself the target of a group of menacing teenage thugs who were pointing at me and yelling:

"You killed our Lord."

Their faces were red with rage as they chanted it over and over.

"It was your *lot* who killed our Lord," one boy yelled, louder and more menacing than the rest.

Up until that point, I hadn't realized I had a "lot," and had no idea what they meant or why I was the focus of their attack. Then it hit me. Their Lord was Jesus Christ, and the "lot" they blamed were the Jews. Putting two and two together, I realized that as a Jew named Goldstone, I was apparently responsible for the death of Jesus Christ.

"You don't really think I killed Jesus?" I blurted out with equal parts fear and disbelief. And with that, I received my first ever punch in the face. I had never been hit by anyone before and, admittedly, was more stunned than hurt. I felt my nose start to bleed and I ran off toward the office of the school headmaster, Derek Bracewell, to report the attack.

After stopping my nosebleed, cleaning myself up, and explaining what had happened, I was shocked again, but this time by the headmaster's response.

"Everyone is entitled to his own opinion, just ignore them," he told me matter-of-factly.

"But his opinion is that I killed Jesus," I shot back.

He looked at me, annoyed at my audacity. "Look, just forget it and try to make friends with the other boys. We have quite a few Jewish pupils, so you should fit in nicely. We even have a daily Jewish prayer assembly every morning in the music teacher's room," he told me, adding that the music teacher was himself a

Jew, as if that piece of information would calm my frustration.

For the next few years I tried to keep as low a profile as I could and avoided eye contact with anyone who looked like they might believe I was capable of killing the son of God.

Then, at sixteen, my life changed. In 1977, I found an advertisement for a trainee sports reporter at the Manchester-based Jewish Gazette. I had long ago decided I wanted to be a journalist, and this seemed like a perfect starting point. But there would be two key challenges to overcome: first, I was sixteen and still in school; and second, I knew absolutely nothing about sports.

The following week was our school Careers Day, and I decided to discuss my plan with our advisor, Elliott Weisberg. Careers in journalism didn't exactly come up often in my school. Pupils were generally encouraged to look at vocational futures such as welding, plumbing, construction, and the armed forces, with an occasional boy scraping through to a second level university.

I sat down with Mr. Weisberg and excitedly told him that I had decided on a career in journalism. I explained that I had found an entry level job and was going to apply for it immediately, as I wanted to be a journalist.

His answer was short and to the point. "Well, you can't," he said.

He then lectured me on more suitable professions for someone with my background and educational ability. He told me that it would take years of study and an academic discipline beyond what I had displayed during my years at this school. If I studied hard, he explained, I might be accepted to a local polytechnic or perhaps even a modest college. As he continued to speak, I stood up, turned away, and left.

I still had almost a year left at the school, but made up my mind as I stormed out of his office that I would get the job as a trainee reporter and everything else would fall into place. I decided that I wouldn't mention my age during the interview unless I was

47

pressed, and wouldn't tell anyone at home or at school until it was a done deal. How difficult could it be?

I went straight to my aunt's house and called the editor (we didn't have a phone of our own at that time). He seemed interested to meet me and we made an appointment to meet that Friday at the paper's Cheetham Hill offices, just a mile or two from Manchester City center.

I told no one about the meeting, not even my parents. Fortunately for me, I looked older. I may not have been academically smart, but I was street smart and could talk a great talk and had mastered the art of *chutzpah*. I convinced myself the job was already mine, and was already planning how to spend my first paycheck.

Friday came around quickly and I put on what I thought were my most grown-up clothes: a plaid blue cardigan, black pants, and a pair of freshly polished lace-up shoes. And with that, I took my first steps toward being a journalist.

On entering the newsroom of the *Jewish Gazette*, the first thing that struck me about the editor, Arthur Sunderland, was that he was a bald man. That was really his only discernible feature. Everything else about him was perfectly forgettable apart from this shiny, overly tanned, bald head.

My meeting with the editor went well. We talked about the job of a trainee reporter, we talked working hours and duties, and we briefly talked about pay. By the end of an hour, I knew I had talked my way into the job.

Only two obstacles remained: the minimum age for the job was eighteen, and I knew nothing whatsoever about sports. I didn't play sports, and I didn't understand the rules of any major (or minor) sport. But I wasn't going to let that stand in my way.

"Do you really have to ask if I like sports?" I said during the interview when asked about my sports knowledge. "Would I be applying to be a sports reporter if I didn't live, eat, and breathe sports?"

That seemed to do the trick. The editor nodded in agreement at the ridiculousness of his question.

Then there was my age. Maybe I wasn't totally honest about that either. I never said I was eighteen; I just didn't say I wasn't. I somehow danced my way around the issue by changing the topic and asking about the pay. That topic made the editor noticeably uncomfortable.

"We pay our trainees a pound a week for every year of their age, so we would start you at eighteen pounds," he said, looking down at the floor.

Now I may have only been a schoolboy, but even I knew that a pound for every year of your age seemed low. At that rate, it would take until I was a pensioner to earn something like a normal wage. For a second, I waited for him to smile and tell me the real salary, but he didn't smile. The offer was for eighteen pounds a week.

"If you're okay with that and free to start, why don't we give you a three-month trial starting on Monday?" he said.

I accepted his offer. In the space of two short hours, I had officially become a journalist. Admittedly, I was a trainee, and on a three-month trial, and making only eighteen pounds a week, but I knew that once I got my feet under the desk there, they would never let me go. And even if they did, I could always start another job when I really was eighteen.

I had one more stop to make on the way home from the interview. I timed my arrival just as Heys Boys' School was breaking for the day and made my way to the headmaster's office. His secretary indicated he was available and I knocked on his office door. His office had always been a place of terror for most pupils, myself included.

Throughout my years there, I had heard the horror stories

of his office canings on the back of the hand. Shockingly, I had managed to get away without being corporally punished, mostly through some quick talk.

Now I was standing in front of him once again, but this time I felt nerves of a different kind.

"I am leaving today," I told the stunned headmaster.

"I have found a job and I'm starting on Monday. Oh, and by the way, your careers advisor told me that I could never be a journalist. Please tell him he was wrong. As of now, I'm a journalist."

And with that I turned and slammed his office door behind me, never to set foot in that school again.

Chapter Seven

The Greatest

I worked for the *Jewish Gazette* for almost three years and during that time eventually confessed to the editor my true age. While he was somewhat surprised, by then I was so much a part of the team he seemed not to care, and in fact agreed to send me to journalism college part-time so I could learn the academic as well as the practical side of the profession.

Even so, I soon began to outgrow the small newsroom. Eventually, I found a new job as a reporter in a much bigger, local newspaper, the *Bury Times*. Although the move gave me more experience, it still wasn't enough to satisfy my ambitions. That would happen a year or two later when I landed a job at the *Birmingham Evening Mail*.

I was still a mainstream news reporter there, but I took every opportunity to cover the celebrity and entertainment beat, which was the domain of Geoff Baker, a manic workaholic. Geoff would later find fame as Paul McCartney's high-profile personal publicist. Baker often gave me entertainment stories to work on with him and it whet my appetite for the world of show business.

While working in Birmingham, I made the strategic change from print to broadcasting—albeit radio broadcasting. I was invited for an interview by the head of independent radio station BRMB. I was up for a new challenge, and I went along to their Aston studios.

It seemed like another world, a technical world of tapes, editing tools, and recording booths. I was a confirmed luddite and could barely operate a car, let alone a recording studio, but I was assured that in a few months it would all become second nature.

It was a quick audition; they had me read from a news script. It didn't seem that difficult and I came back into the newsroom all smiles. They told me I had the job; however, there was one big problem.

"You can't say the word 'one' correctly," said the news editor, Brian Sheppard.

How many ways could there be to say "one?" I thought.

"You pronounce 'one' like 'wonn' because you're from Manchester. We need a neutral pronunciation, so it would be more like 'wun' or even 'wan'," he told me—adding that until I could say that word correctly, I would never be allowed to read a news bulletin on his station. The importance of that one word soon became obvious: the big news bulletin of the day was always at one o'clock and connections to the M1 motorway were just up the road from the studios.

Nevertheless, I started as a broadcast journalist the following week, and for the next two months spent every spare moment practicing my "wun" and "wan" to the annoyance of every person around me.

Although I was a news reporter, whenever possible, I looked for entertainment stories. I would soon get my big break from a legend: a man simply called "The Greatest."

As unlikely as it might seem, a local youth center in Birmingham's predominantly black neighborhood of Handsworth had invited boxing legend Muhammad Ali to visit their new premises. Improbably, Ali said yes.

Determined to cover the event, I assigned myself. I befriended the visit organizers well in advance, and by the time Ali set foot in Birmingham, I had all but moved into the building. I commandeered the radio station's trusty old news car for the duration of his visit, and set up a mini studio inside it to broadcast into the station's regular news and talk programs.

I was also required to call into the station's main sports programs, which were fronted by the legendary Tony Butler. Tony was an institution among radio sports commentators; he was passionate, insane, and always controversial. He was a huge Ali fan and not happy that I had cornered the market in station coverage. But I promised him I would deliver an interview with the champ. I admit I didn't know exactly how I was going to achieve that.

On the first day of Ali's visit, hundreds of local fans turned out to welcome him to their neglected community. The champ smiled broadly, waved, and shook hands as he was ushered inside. He was scheduled to spend two days in the area, so I knew I had a bit of time to secure an interview.

I approached Ali during a break on that first afternoon. He was bigger than I imagined, both in size and personality. His smile was infectious and seemed truly genuine, and he oozed warmth and charisma whenever he spoke. I asked him how he was enjoying being a part of this revitalized neighborhood.

Ali told me that he had not had much time to get acquainted with the people or the place, which I took to mean "now go away and don't bother me again," but I was wrong.

"Why don't you come back tomorrow and do an interview with me and I will answer all your questions?" said Ali.

The radio station seemed shocked that I had managed to get even a few words on tape from Ali and suggested I declare victory and forget about returning the next morning. I told them that I had been promised a full sit-down interview by Ali, even though

I didn't really believe this myself. Hopefully, I would get at least a few words the station could use. Tony Butler had collared me on the way out and joked that I should bring Ali into the studio tomorrow to appear live on his sports show. Wouldn't that be a worldwide coup? he laughed. I ignored him, and prayed that Ali would show up.

The next day, I returned to the youth center a few hours before Ali was due to arrive. I talked with kids who had met their hero, and with parents who now felt proud to call this run-down neighborhood their home. The atmosphere was electric, with the kids in a virtual frenzy and their parents equally excited as we waited for the champ to arrive. But there was no sign of Ali. Even though I had convinced myself that he definitely would not show up for this interview, a part of me secretly hoped he would. I felt crushed.

About an hour later than planned, Ali's car pulled up and the champ stepped out to be surrounded again by hundreds of smiling faces.

I was near the entrance hoping to at least grab a quick word as he passed me. I had my tape recorder ready to pounce, but he noticed my microphone and just carried on walking. This did not seem promising. He shook hands with some local dignitaries and then walked over to a boxing ring and looked at the youngsters training.

I approached him nervously, microphone held out gingerly, like a piece of precious metal. I was a moment away from asking him about the interview, when I surprised myself and switched gears. "Shall we go then?" I said.

"Go?" asked Ali.

"Yes. Remember you agreed to do a sit-down interview today with my radio station? Didn't I mention that we were hoping to surprise our listeners by having you live in the studio instead of on tape?" I bluffed.

There were only two ways this situation could have ended, and one of them involved me being punched by the greatest boxer of all time.

"You got a car?" said Ali.

And that is how I came to drive Muhammad Ali, the greatest boxer in history, to my radio station, in a tiny beat-up dirty Ford hatchback.

We arrived just in time to surprise Tony Butler live on the air and give BRMB a world exclusive one-hour studio interview and call-in with the champ. Decades later, my news editor Brian Sheppard commented on my Facebook page that I had "More front than Brighton"—a reference to England's seaside resort of Brighton and its long boardwalk and sea front.

Throughout the interview, Ali compulsively scribbled and drew pictures on pieces of scrap paper. As he finished each doodle, he would write a phrase or little poem on the scrap of paper and then hand it to me. Some were for me, some I passed on to the news staff. Before he left, he posed for photos with some young fans who had come to the station to meet him.

To this day I cherish a photo of me and Ali at the station with one of those young fans; it is a constant reminder to me that anything is possible. You just have to believe in yourself…and hope not to get punched.

Chapter Eight

Down To the Wire

The Miss Universe pageant of 2013 was set to take place at Crocus City Hall, Moscow, on the evening of Saturday, November 9th. But before any of the eighty-six contestants had a chance to set foot on Russian soil, an unexpected controversy threatened to derail the pageant. Just months earlier, the Russian government had sparked worldwide outrage with the passing of its so-called *gay propaganda law*, "for the Purpose of Protecting Children from Information Advocating for a Denial of Traditional Family Values."

The bill, which was signed by President Putin in June of that year, was immediately condemned by human rights organizations around the globe, and seen as an attack on the Russian LGBT community. It was also cited as a cause of an increasing wave of anti-gay violence that was sweeping across Russia.

That year's expected telecast hosts, Bravo's Andy Cohen and E!'s Giuliana Rancic, refused to participate. Cohen told E! News that he would be "concerned for his safety" if he attended the pageant in Russia.

Paula Shugart was expressly clear that her paramount consideration was for the safety of her staff, contestants, and Miss Universe visitors. Many involved in working on the event were gay, and Paula confided to me that some of her staff feared being arrested or physically attacked if they set foot in Moscow.

She was adamant to distance the pageant from all aspects of the new legislation and an official statement was issued saying that the law was "diametrically opposed to the core values" of the Miss Universe Organization.

After I explained to Emin the seriousness of the problem, he personally assured me, then Paula and her team, that the Agalarovs would provide additional security to ensure everyone involved in the event felt safe and, more importantly, was safe.

Emin was sure the issue was being overblown by the Western media. Although he had many friends who were gay, they were successful and rich and therefore cocooned in an impenetrable bubble of wealth, privilege, and protection.

When the hosts of the pageant were finally named, both had strong connections to the LGBT community: former Spice Girl Mel B, and openly gay TV anchor Thomas Roberts.

Roberts announced that he would bring his husband, Patrick Abner, to Moscow with him and they would walk the red carpet together. I hoped this would send a positive message to the LGBT community in Russia and around the world. To emphasize his point and affirm his commitment, Roberts wore a bright pink suit on the red carpet, where he posed for photos with Abner in front of the world's media.

"Boycotting and vilifying from the outside is too easy. Rather, I choose to offer my support of the LGBT community in Russia by going to Moscow and hosting this event as a journalist, an anchor, and a man who happens to be gay," Roberts said.

In another unexpected twist, the runner-up that year, Spain's Patricia Yurena Rodriguez Alonso, would come out as gay the following year when she posted a photograph of herself with her girlfriend to Instagram with the caption "Romeo and Juliet."

The contestants began arriving in Moscow three weeks before the pageant. Each was hoping to win a crown and jumpstart a career, but the stakes were high for all of us. I felt particularly invested in the event's success; after all, I was the one who had convinced Aras to go ahead with the multimillion-dollar project.

Although later there would be speculation that the Kremlin initiated the pageant to bring Donald Trump to Russia, or that Trump had conceived it to gain entree to the Russian business world, in reality the pageant was happening because of Emin's spontaneous idea. Unlike governments in other countries that had hosted Miss Universe, the Russian government didn't appear to back the event at all.

There was no financial support or sponsorship by any official government entity. In fact, when we tried to film segments for the broadcast in Red Square to promote Moscow to the world, we were asked to pay a location fee. This seemed outrageous to me. The very best of Moscow would be highlighted throughout the two-hour worldwide broadcast, and yet the Kremlin appeared indifferent and oblivious to what we were bringing to the country's capital. We pushed back against the fee successfully, but I was taken aback that officials seemed to be, at best, indifferent to the success of the pageant.

Eventually, I learned that one reason for this indifference was that the government was racing to finish the Winter Olympics site in Sochi, and viewed Miss Universe as a distraction and even a nuisance. While the Russian government may have cold-shouldered the contest, the people of Moscow embraced it warmly and we were met with cheering crowds and nonstop major Russian media coverage wherever we went.

During the final ten days of rehearsals, we organized dozens of social and media events to create excitement among the contestants and for broadcast. Among the standout events were a national costume parade on the mezzanine of Emin's newly opened Vegas Mall, and a charity fundraising night in which Moscow's rich and famous bid on items brought by each of the eighty-six contestants. I had no plans to buy anything, but as the items kept selling, I got caught up in the excitement, raised my hand, and instead of buying what I thought was a souvenir scrap of metal from the Panama Canal's construction, I ended up the proud owner of a VIP box at Crocus City Hall, something I'd presumably have access to anyway.

But the icing on the cake for everyone would be the arrival of Donald Trump, who was viewed by the Russian public with a wild enthusiasm that could almost be compared to the popularity of their own leader, Vladimir Putin. And that was saying a lot. The Russian President's popularity at the time was overwhelming, with the international media reporting a more than eighty percent approval rating.

A couple of years later I would learn why Putin's appeal went far beyond politics. I was having lunch in St. Petersburg with a translator and her colleagues, and she told me a fascinating story. She said many Russians, especially followers of the Orthodox Church, believed that the assassination of Czar Nicholas and the Romanov family in July of 1918 during the Russian Revolution resulted in a curse being placed over the nation. This curse, she said, had plagued the country ever since with endless hardships and suffering.

She told me that these same believers, who number in the tens of millions, are convinced that Vladimir Putin broke that curse when he came to power, returning Russia to its "rightful place" as a dominant power and influential world leader.

I wasn't sure what to make of this explanation, but the more I thought about it, the more it strangely made sense. There was a kind of Grimm's fairy tale quality to the story, and it provided something of an insight into the thinking of the everyday Russian people I was now working among.

While Russians proudly see themselves as logical and pragmatic, so much of their culture and identity is still grounded in superstition and folklore. *Could this old wives' tale about Putin have more truth in it for the people of this vast country than even they might care to admit?*

Whatever the cause of Putin's popularity, the lack of support from his government was putting enormous financial pressure on us to keep costs down. Not only was the government not supporting the contest, but we were getting less than anticipated support from the private sector as well. Normally, there is anywhere from twelve to eighteen months between the announcement of the host city and the contest. However, because Emin had bullied his idea through, we only had six months from the announcement to the event. That made it considerably harder to get vendors on board, and in fact we had only a few.

I had by now become the bridge between all parties involved in this incredibly complex and demanding beauty pageant. The Miss Universe creative team had ambitious ideas and expensive needs. The Russian Crocus team wanted to keep the budget in check. And I was caught in the middle of the "must have" requirements of one team, and the "must cut" pragmatic concerns of the other.

During that time, my point of contact for all things related to finances and sponsorships on the project was Ike Kaveladze. He and I spent endless hours trying to keep the budget from spiraling out of control, trimming costs whenever and wherever we could, and discussing creative ways to attract potential sponsors for the pageant.

In addition to the financial issues, I was constantly bombarded with questions from both sides, ranging from the weight-bearing load capacity of the Crocus City Hall roof, to the possibility of having construction crews begin work an hour or two later each morning, since construction noise was waking the Miss Universe staff up too early in their adjoining hotel rooms. One staff member told me she had resorted to sleeping in her bathtub to avoid the noise each morning from her bedroom window.

One moment Emin was telling me we needed to chop the budget by millions of dollars, and the next moment Paula was telling me her broadcast team needed expensive outside broadcast vans, which were only available thousands of miles away in Germany.

Eventually, Emin decided he could offset some of these additional costs by shooting a new music video during the final days of the contest. To keep the budget down, he would use his sprawling mansion on the Agalarov estate, just outside Moscow, as the location for the video shoot.

The song for the video "In Another Life" would also be one of the tracks Emin would perform live during the Miss Universe telecast.

"Do you think you could get, say, a dozen of the contestants to be in the music video?" he asked me during dinner one night.

I was doubtful since there was hardly a spare minute to be found in the packed rehearsal and promotional schedule set by the producers in the run up to the big event.

"Paula will never agree. It would take them away from their rehearsals for a whole day," I said, hoping to talk him out of the idea, and save myself another headache.

Emin poured himself a glass of his favorite Chivas whisky and told me, "Let's just plan it anyway. I know you'll find a way to get the contestants there."

It was another example of his "plan it now and then ask later" approach to life. I, as usual, was assigned the role of the one doing the asking. There were only three days left to convince Paula and her team of the importance of allowing a dozen contestants to be cast in the video shoot. I knew I had to pick my moment carefully.

There was, as usual, no plan B from Emin; I had to make certain plan A worked.

Paula, fortunately, had come from the world of live events and TV production and was used to outlandish, last minute requests and changes. She was tough and stood her ground when she needed to, but she also knew when to give a little.

"We could maybe make this work, but you will have to select random contestants in order to fit in with their specific schedules," she said.

"Done," I replied.

As long as they had a sash and smiled, I didn't care if they were from Venus or Mars. Emin had asked only for a dozen or so contestants; he hadn't specified nationalities.

Eventually, we managed to secure contestants from a range of countries that included the US, Russia, Switzerland, Puerto Rico, Ukraine, Philippines, Spain, and Japan. The diverse contestants added a truly international flavor to the dream sequences in the video and Emin and the director were delighted with the result.

The next day, as we watched some of the footage, we both agreed that although the contestants were fun, there was something missing. The video needed a strong opening and closing, and we definitely didn't yet have it yet.

"What if you got Donald Trump to be in the video?" asked Emin.

"Are you demented?" I said.

"No, it's a great idea. What if we did a scene from *The Apprentice*?" Emin added, becoming more and more animated in his excitement over this idea.

"Sure. And why doesn't he fire you at the end?" I shot back sarcastically.

"That's it! I'll be daydreaming and Trump can fire me. It's perfect. Rob, make it happen," said a now excited Emin.

I looked over at his smiling face and knew there was no point arguing about logistics or anything like that. It was another done deal in Emin's head.

But I did tell Emin that this time he should definitely work on a plan B.

"We don't need a plan B. I know you'll get him to do it. He likes you and it's a great idea. I'll deal with the logistics," he assured me.

It was classic Emin flattery. I had spent barely a few hours with Trump alongside Emin at the Las Vegas dinner, yet according to Emin, Trump liked me! It was ridiculous, but I knew that, like everything, I would somehow make it work.

A couple of days before Donald Trump was due to leave for Moscow, Paula pulled me aside to let me know that his schedule had changed. He would now be arriving one day later than planned, and that he would be flying home right after the contest. She told me the reason for the shortened visit was that Trump was going to attend famed evangelist Billy Graham's ninety-fifth birthday celebration in North Carolina.

That meant we would essentially only have Trump in Moscow for a day and a half: part of Friday, all of Saturday, and the early hours of Sunday morning.

The good news was that Trump had assured Paula that he would get some rest on the long flight to Russia and he would be ready to start working the moment he landed. This was good to hear, because Emin's team had a packed media and promotional schedule set up for him and I didn't want to be the one to start canceling events.

Trump would fly to Moscow on a private jet owned by his friend, casino mogul Phil Ruffin, who would accompany Trump on the visit with his wife Oleksandra, a former Miss Ukraine in the 2004 Miss Universe pageant.

When I told Emin that Trump was arriving later, he was only concerned that we did not have to cancel any important events.

But he didn't mention either the music video shoot I was supposed to get Trump to agree to be in nor the huge birthday dinner for Aras that was set for the night before the pageant. Of course, as far as Emin was concerned, these were done deals, set in stone.

All I could do now, however, was to wait for Donald Trump to arrive in Moscow for a thirty-six-hour visit that, years later, would become another important piece in the RussiaGate puzzle.

Chapter Nine

The Showman Cometh

My first glimpse of Donald Trump in Moscow was on a miserable, overcast Friday evening in front of Nobu restaurant. Nobu is situated in a building owned by Emin in one of the city's most fashionable shopping districts whose storefronts reflect Russia's moneyed class. Prada, Louis Vuitton, and Hermes stand proudly on immaculate streets with old-fashioned street lamps, lighting the way for impeccably dressed shoppers.

I was discovering that the inner sanctum of moneyed Moscow operates as a virtual gated community for the rich and powerful. Many Muscovites say that the only time average Russians enter this exclusive bastion of privilege and wealth is to get to work as shop assistants, restaurant workers, or domestic help. It's the Rodeo Drive or Fifth Avenue of Russia, a place where a pair of designer shoes can easily cost more than the average monthly salary of most of the country's workers.

Emin and I joined Aras out in front to greet Trump, who was all smiles as he exited his fortified Mercedes. He seemed excited to have received a presidential-style police escort into the city, something Aras arranged and which is afforded to only the most important of VIPs and visiting heads of state. Throughout his stay in Moscow, Trump would be escorted by police outriders to make sure he was delayed as little as possible by Moscow's notoriously congested traffic.

He shook hands first with Aras and then with Emin before he turned to me. He patted me on the shoulder, and said it was great to be in Moscow for what he knew would be an "amazing" event.

Trump apologized to us for arriving a day later than originally scheduled, but explained, as Paula had already told me, that he had been to Billy Graham's birthday the night before. He said it had been important for him to be there, but didn't elaborate. I didn't understand why Trump was attending the famous preacher's birthday until several years later when he announced he was running for president and began targeting the evangelical vote.

We walked Trump into the waiting elevator which led directly to the second floor restaurant, where more than twenty of Russia's most important banking and business leaders were waiting to meet him. I hadn't been involved in organizing this event, so I knew only that the group was headed by one of the country's most powerful and influential financial figures, Herman Gref, a former Minister of Economics and Trade, now CEO of Sberbank, Russia's largest bank.

These sobering men appeared almost giddy with excitement as Trump entered the room with a smile as broad as the Brooklyn Bridge. He seemed in his element going around shaking hands and heaping praise on his hosts, the Agalarovs. Trump kept repeating the phrase he had used when he first met Aras and Emin in Las Vegas, "These are the richest men in Russia." He seemed to enjoy using this phrase as much to bolster his own status as to elevate his hosts' importance.

It was then that the formal introduction took place, with Emin acting as host and translator. He said a few brief words praising Trump as both a groundbreaking mogul and one of the world's most dynamic business brands, and then invited some of the guests to ask Trump questions.

One of those present asked Trump his view on the Russian economy, and another for his opinion of President Putin and his leadership. Trump heaped praise on the country's business leaders, who he said were responsible for the current economic boom in Russia. He called it "very impressive." He went on to talk about his personal admiration for Vladimir Putin, who he said was a "tough" leader, unlike America's own President Obama, who was, he said, "weak."

Gref would later tell Bloomberg News that he found Trump to be "a sensible person, very lively in his responses, with a positive energy and a good attitude toward Russia."

But a real moment of Trump *chutzpah* came when one of the guests asked him his view on the current European debt crisis in light of Greece's recent bailout. Trump rose to his feet, paused, and with an air of confidence and authority said that before answering that question, he wanted to speak about something of which he was very proud: the success of his TV show, *The Apprentice*.

He explained how it had become a huge success not just in America, but around the world, and discovered lots of smart and savvy business people, and generated lots of income for his media partner NBC, which, coincidentally, was also the co-owner of the Miss Universe pageant.

"It's a big money earner for NBC and is consistently the number one rated show in its time slot," he told his audience, who, if they were waiting to hear his views on the current European economic crisis, would wait in vain.

And with that, Trump ended the discussion, thanked his audience for coming, and said he looked forward to seeing them all at the pageant the next day. The group of powerful businessmen and oligarchs rose to their feet and gave Trump a standing ovation.

The closest Donald Trump had come to mentioning Europe, let alone a debt crisis, was telling his audience how *The Apprentice* was shown throughout the European continent. And yet these powerful bankers and businessmen could not get enough of him. As Trump moved throughout the room, he stopped from time to time, presumably to make small talk with his guests.

Trump stayed for ten more minutes to pose for photos and lap up the adulation until it was time for him to leave so as to stay on our tight schedule.

I will never forget this reception in Moscow and how Trump had charmed a room of the sternest, most powerful, most serious looking Russians I've ever seen with his bravado and showmanship. This would form the basis of my opinion of what Russia and its all-important leaders thought of Donald Trump when I wrote about it in my 2016 email to Don Jr.

Trump said a final goodbye to the group, and Emin and I got into the elevator with him and Keith Schiller. I decided this was probably the best moment I was going to get to ask Trump a question even more important than what to do about the Greek debt crisis.

I looked straight at him and said: "I have a crazy thing to ask. We're shooting a music video early tomorrow morning for Emin's new single, and there's a part where he's in a boardroom meeting and falls asleep daydreaming. We wondered if you would be in it, and fire him like you do in *The Apprentice*," I said, hoping my reference would flatter him enough to get him to agree to my request.

I braced myself for rejection. This was yet another one of those moments that Emin was always getting me into.

"If you can shoot my part in fifteen minutes, I am in," Trump said.

"Mr. Trump, we will do it in thirteen," interjected a beaming Emin from out of nowhere.

As we walked Trump outside to his waiting car, he turned to

me and, hinting at what had just happened inside at the reception, said, "Has there ever been a better self-promoter than Donald Trump?"

I have always been fascinated by the *chutzpah* of people who speak of themselves in the third person. It's insane yet at the same time, fabulous and takes a certain kind of person to carry it off. I had seen it firsthand many times among the rich and famous, most notably, when as a young reporter, I was sent early one morning to grab a sound bite from UK Prime Minister Margaret Thatcher.

As she stepped out of a helicopter, I approached her and her aides with a tape recorder, shouting to them over the noise of the rotor blades: "Would Mrs. Thatcher speak into this microphone for a quick interview?"

I will never forget her response.

"My dear," she replied, "if it's good publicity, Mrs Thatcher would speak into a hairbrush."

Two polarizing, world-class media figures (and their world-class egos) using self-deprecating charm to win people over, and both speaking of themselves in the third person.

Once Trump had agreed to be in the video, I knew I needed to let the video director know as soon as possible. I could already picture the blood draining from his face. He always pulled out all the stops for Emin's video shoots, but this was going to need more than skill. It would need perfect timing and a lot of luck to set up two scenes so they could be shot in fifteen minutes.

Still, I had done my part and got Emin his star power. Now, all we had to do was shoot Trump's part in less time than it takes most people to shower.

"We can't possibly shoot this in fifteen minutes," director Yuri confided in me. "It can't be done."

"What about thirteen?" I said half-jokingly. "That's what Emin promised him."

The director and his team worked throughout the night to create two separate shooting areas in the boardroom of the Ritz Carlton Hotel. Trump's shoot was scheduled for 8 a.m. the next morning, all he had to do was come down in the elevator from his suite and be ready to film on time. I would write a simple script for him.

I knew that once we had Trump safely on set, I could probably stretch that fifteen minutes, but not by much. His schedule for the next day was already packed with a huge media conference, the red carpet, the pageant and the VIP after party. After all that, he planned to leave directly for the airport and fly back to the US.

After the Nobu reception, Trump was scheduled to make a quick pit stop at the Ritz Carlton to freshen up and then leave for Crocus City, where he would check out the Miss Universe venue and then attend Aras's birthday celebration dinner.

Crocus City is about sixteen miles from the center of Moscow and reached via the always busy MKAD ring road. Along with its shopping and leisure facilities, it also houses Emin's restaurant Backstage, which would be the setting for his father's 58th birthday party.

Almost five hundred guests, including many of Russia's richest, most famous and celebrated citizens, would attend this glittering occasion. But even though the guests were ostensibly there to toast Aras, we all knew that the most intense focus of interest would be Aras's guest, Donald Trump.

After confirming that Trump would attend the star-studded birthday party, I had another daunting task: getting all of the Miss Universe contestants to surprise Aras on stage at the stroke of midnight to sing "Happy Birthday" and make a special presentation to him. If all went according to plan, it would be a moment to remember for the Agalarov patriarch, but the logistics were complicated. The contestants had to have enough time to finish their dress rehearsal, get changed, and make it to the party on time.

And while I would have one eye on the contestants, I would have the other firmly on Donald Trump. I needed to ensure that he didn't get bored or tired and decide to head back to his hotel and leave the party early before the big reveal. And although I needed him to party the night away with the Agalarovs, I also needed him to be well rested and on time early the next morning to make his all-important cameo in Emin's music video.

My secret weapon in all this was Trump's stamina. He showed no signs of tiredness as he joined the hundreds of guests in toasting Aras's birthday, and as the clock struck midnight, a giant birthday cake was wheeled out. Before blowing out the candles, Aras was feted by his family, friends, and many of the famous celebrity faces in the room, who made speeches and toasted his business achievements and success. Trump stood and applauded each speech to the delight of his oligarch host, who beamed at the adulation from his friends, family, and colleagues in the room.

Finally, Aras blew out the birthday candles. That was my signal to bring out all eighty-six glamorous contestants, along with a giant framed photograph of them with Aras and Emin in the middle. The framed photo, which they had all signed, was huge and it took at least a dozen of the women to carry it. I thought I saw Aras mist up; he appeared genuinely touched as he thanked them all for making his birthday a night he would never forget.

It was then Emin's chance to surprise his dad and he performed a small concert, which included his father's favorite operatic song made famous by Emin's mentor, the late Muslim Magomayev. The song "Blue Eternity" drew a standing ovation from the room. One guest seemed especially impressed with Emin's performance that night. "Wow! You can really sing. I never knew you could sing like that," exclaimed Donald Trump loudly to the delight of both the singer and his proud father.

It was after one in the morning when Trump finally said his

goodbyes and left Crocus City for the hotel. He was accompanied, as always, by Keith Schiller and members of Emin's security detail. His trip back to the Ritz Carlton would take about thirty minutes thanks to the ever-present police outriders. For the rest of us, it would take upwards of an hour.

I planned to give Keith a call at around 7 a.m. to make sure Trump was awake and ready to shoot his scene for the video. Trump had been on the go since landing in Moscow a little over twelve hours earlier, and I was acutely aware that he had flown overnight from the States. He would have a packed day today, Saturday, with media interviews, a huge press conference, red carpet photos, and the pageant itself. He was also scheduled to attend the thousand-person after party following the crowning of the winner, and there he would once again be the center of attention. Then, as we all went to bed, he would be whisked to the airport to get on the private jet back to New York.

Years later, this overnight stay at the Ritz Carlton Hotel would come under intense scrutiny after the publication of the so-called Steele dossier, which contained a claim that Trump had hired prostitutes to urinate on each other in his hotel suite—on the same bed where President and Mrs. Obama had slept during their visit to Moscow.

There has been a lot of speculation about how Trump himself insisted on staying in this particular hotel suite because of its Obama provenance.

The reality, however, is that up until a few days before his arrival in Moscow, there had been a very good chance Trump wouldn't even be staying in the Ritz. To accommodate all the judges and our VIP guests, we had been working with a different hotel partner, which owned several brands including the InterContinental Hotel, Crowne Plaza, and Holiday Inn. Their flagship InterContinental Hotel in Moscow was definitely a luxury property, but considerably less ritzy than the Ritz and much less expensive. At that point, cost was an issue. Emin was trying his best to save money wherever possible in the constantly increasing pageant budget, and he and I had gone back and forth right up until the last moment over where Trump and Keith Schiller would stay. I had heard that the cost of top luxury suites at the Ritz Carlton during this period could easily reach twenty thousand dollars a night.

Still, I knew I couldn't let Emin book Trump into a lesser hotel, just to save a few thousand dollars. I told him that we had to put Trump up in the Ritz. Anything less would mean getting things off on the wrong foot with Trump. Emin agreed. So a few days before Trump was due to arrive, we finally confirmed a suite at the Ritz. At no time did I personally specify which luxury suite they should give Trump, but at the time, I assumed the hotel would upgrade this particular VIP guest to their highest possible category of accommodation.

Years later, when I saw media reports of the alleged salacious "pee" episode at the Ritz Carlton, it came as a total shock. I had heard nothing, not even a whisper of something like this occurring during Trump's time in Moscow. In general, I was constantly told details about everything, including all the gossip surrounding the pageant, so I would have expected something as scandalous as prostitutes peeing on each other in Trump's suite to have reached my ears.

As far as what has been alleged, I don't know if it happened or not. In theory, anything is possible, but as far as I was aware, on the night in question, Trump should have been getting five or six hours of much needed sleep in order to be ready for our video shoot early that morning, which would then be followed by an extremely long day, and even longer night in front of the world's media. It has been reported extensively that Trump only sleeps about four hours a night, so I was confident he would be up bright and early for our filming.

Whatever did or did not occur in Trump's Ritz Carlton suite in the early hours of November 9th, by 7 a.m., our video shoot was ready to go in an *Apprentice*-style "boardroom" that we had created on the mezzanine level of the hotel.

As soon as Emin and the other actors were in their seats, I called Keith and asked him to bring his boss down so we could start the scene. Trump came down a few minutes later looking rested and dressed in a business suit. He shook hands with the crew and actors and asked that we start. Trump had not yet seen a script, although I had written one. When I offered it to him, he said he would simply make it up as he went along. He was going to wing it.

Trump's cameo role was straightforward. The premise of the video was that Emin's character is in a boardroom meeting with a group of colleagues sitting around a conference table when he begins daydreaming. In his imagination, the various Miss Universe contestants appear as if by magic during his everyday activities. Emin is awakened suddenly and finds himself face to face with none other than Donald Trump in a scene reminiscent of the boardroom endings of *The Apprentice*.

The scene had to be done in one or two takes at the most, if we were to keep to the schedule, which I had assured Trump we would do.

As the cameras rolled, Trump told the assembled boardroom sternly: "Wake him up right now. Emin, wake up, c'mon. What's wrong with you? What's wrong with you, Emin? Emin, get with it, you're always late, you're just another pretty face. I'm really tired of you. You're fired!"

We shot this scene from every conceivable angle simultaneously as our director knew there was no going back or bringing our guest star in for re-shoots. The minutes were ticking away, and I was well aware that I had told Trump that this would be a wrap within fifteen minutes. I just hoped he hadn't taken Emin's offer seriously to shoot it all in thirteen.

I saw Trump check the time at one point and I shot a desperate glance to the director, but our star stuck with us and despite the shoot running over by about twenty additional minutes, he seemed happy.

Finally, I had done all my crazy "asks" and I could concentrate on the contest itself, which was less than twelve hours away. There would be no more distractions...or so I thought.

Just as Trump was leaving the boardroom, he turned to me and dropped his own bombshell. He asked if I had heard whether President Putin would be attending the show that night, and if not, if there was at least a chance that he could still meet with him.

There had been rumblings of a possible meeting between the two for weeks but nothing so far had come of it. The subject of such a meeting had first come up during a lunch between me and Paula shortly after Trump had announced the contest would be staged in Moscow.

"Oh God," she had joked. "You know he's going to want to meet with Putin!"

Although it was an off-the-cuff remark, I knew she was probably right, and relayed this to Emin, who said we should take the idea of Trump requesting a meeting with the Russian President seriously. Emin said he would have his father make a formal request through the appropriate official government channels.

Emin asked me to get Paula to ask Trump to prepare a hand-signed letter to President Putin, personally inviting him to attend the pageant. I passed on the request to her, and soon after we received the typed letter. At the bottom of it, Trump had scrawled in pen: "Lots of beautiful women." Presumably this was an attempt to sweeten the invitation, and Trump had tried to personalize the invitation in his own inimitable style.

For weeks I heard nothing about the meeting from anyone, and every time I brought up the subject with Emin his answer was always the same: we have to wait for his father to receive an official response. Emin pointed out that it was highly unlikely Putin would attend the contest; after all, he said, President Obama probably wasn't in the habit of attending beauty pageants either, so it would be understandable if Putin declined the invitation.

Emin continued to believe, however, that there was a chance of some kind of a meeting happening between Trump and Putin. By now though, there was only a very small window in which any meeting could take place. With Trump due to leave Moscow right after the contest, I had about five hours to try to confirm what could undoubtedly be a historic encounter.

I assured Trump that I would check again that morning to see what could be done at least to get him a definitive answer. I asked Emin what the reality was of Putin and Trump meeting that day. He shrugged and said it had been brought up many times, but there was still no official response, and any communication would come via his father.

To me, that meant only more uncertainty, as I didn't imagine for one moment that Aras had such a chummy relationship with President Putin that he could just pick up the phone and say, "Hey, Vlad, time's running out. What's up with this Trump meeting?"

One thing Emin did now know for sure, however, was that President Putin was definitely not planning to attend the pageant itself. He told me that would have involved major security checks of the venue and additional planning, none of which had been requested. So, if there was to be a meeting at all, it would most likely have to take place at the Kremlin in the next few hours.

I was more than a little excited at the prospect of this encounter, not because I cared about the meeting itself, but because I knew that somehow I would end up being able to take the selfie to end all selfies, which would be the jewel in my social media crown. I would instinctively know exactly where to stand during their meeting having spent decades inserting myself directly behind celebrity clients on our red carpets—much to the horror of both the media and my colleagues who work on events with me.

For the next hour or two, I helped Emin pick out his outfits for his live musical performance at the show, but at the back of my mind was the unanswered question about the meeting with Putin.

Emin told me that he was going to give Trump a tour of Crocus City and also get him to sign a star to be placed in their Walkway of Fame at their adjoining shopping mall called Vegas. During the tour, I learned later, Emin had pointed out to Trump the site of a planned residential development, and brought up the idea of possibly branding one of the soon-to-be built apartment blocks as Trump Tower.

His VIP guest must have been excited at the idea, because hours later during the huge Miss Universe press conference, Trump talked about plans for a Trump Tower Moscow. His remarks were picked up by media around the world including in the US, where it made headlines.

The rest of the day was a blur, with a seemingly never-ending barrage of production and last minute scheduling questions being thrown at me. Then, at around three or four in the afternoon, we got word that Putin's official spokesman Dmitry Peskov was going to call Aras with some important information. Emin asked me to make sure to bring Trump to the conference room where Aras would take the call.

No one knew at this stage if Trump was about to be summoned to the Kremlin to meet Putin, but we all gathered in a small room backstage at Crocus City Hall to await the much anticipated call.

We waited, and waited, and then waited some more. Eventually, about forty minutes later than scheduled, Aras's cellphone rang. It was Peskov calling with a message, a message that was so off-the-wall that I would dine out on the story with friends for months when I returned to the United States.

Peskov informed Aras that there could be no meeting with Trump and Putin that day, but the reason wasn't political—it was a matter of royal precedence and unavoidable tardiness.

President Putin, it seemed, was unable to meet Donald Trump because an official audience with the newly crowned king of Holland at the Kremlin was running late as a result of the Dutch king being delayed in traffic. I never found out if this delay was due to air traffic or road traffic, but either way, it meant the window of opportunity for Trump to visit Putin was gone.

Peskov did, however, send a personal invitation from President Putin to meet with Trump at any time in the future, suggesting the upcoming Winter Olympics in Sochi, should Trump be free to attend.

So after all of that anticipation and waiting, there would be no meeting of the minds of these two men, and to my great disappointment, I wouldn't get that all-important selfie.

And why? *Because the King of Holland couldn't get to the Kremlin on time.*

This story would provide some much needed light relief years later during my RussiaGate interview with the Senate Intelligence Committee in Washington DC. It was at the end of a particularly grueling day when one of the staffers who had been leading the questioning took me to one side as I was leaving the room to make an amusing observation.

"You know, you should really send the Dutch king the biggest bunch of flowers you can find. If he had not been delayed that day, and you had been the one who had taken Mr. Trump to meet

President Putin at the Kremlin, imagine how much more awful your life would be right now?"

I laughed out loud and thanked him for his candid insight. But secretly, a part of me knew he was in fact one hundred percent correct. I could only imagine what the media would have made of that Kremlin visit and, of course, my part in it.

It was then that I decided to dedicate this book to His Majesty King Willem-Alexander of the Netherlands for his now much appreciated tardiness on that rainy afternoon in Moscow.

As for the Miss Universe contest, that was won by twenty-five-year-old Venezuelan fashion model, Gabriela "Molly" Isler. She was the seventh Miss Universe from Venezuela, the third in six years. Spain was runner-up, while Ecuador took third place. The winners were chosen by a team of international celebrity judges including supermodel Carol Alt, singer Philipp Kirkorov, Olympic gold medal skater Tara Lipinski, restaurateur Chef Nobu Matsuhisa, and Aerosmith front man Steven Tyler. Among the special guests that night was pop singer Nick Jonas, then-boyfriend of Olivia Culpo.

I spent most of the time at the pageant backstage with Emin preparing for what was unquestionably his most important live performance to date. It would be seen around the world and featured intricate choreography with the contestants crisscrossing the stage. Emin had skipped most of his rehearsals because of his non-stop schedule, and so I was more than a little nervous as he took the stage that night. I think I actually kept my eyes closed for much of the seven-minute performance, opening them only toward the end when I heard the cheer of the audience.

He did a great job. He didn't put a foot wrong, despite hating all choreography. On my way to greet him in his dressing room, I bumped into the choreographer who joked, "He was flawless. Think how incredible he could be if he actually rehearsed."

I passed along her comment to Emin in his dressing room, and his answer was one that stuck with me for many years.

"Rob, I will never let you down."

Chapter Ten

The King and I

As strange as it may sound, the king of Holland wasn't the first king to have an influence on my life.

In 1987, I was living in Australia, working for the Australian Associated Press. I had positioned myself as the go-to reporter for big entertainment stories. When I heard Michael Jackson was coming to Australia as part of his *Bad* tour, I was determined to get an interview with the King of Pop.

Although Jackson rarely spoke to the media, and had a well-documented aversion to journalists and their prying eyes and questions, I begged my editor to let me follow the entire tour, promising I would somehow get access to Michael.

This was Jackson's first solo worldwide tour, and it would go on to become one of the biggest tours of the decade.

I reached out to his Australian publicist, Gaynor Crawford, as well as his American PR guru, the legendary Lee Solters. Somehow I managed to convince both of them that I would file stories day and night, if necessary, as long as I could cover every show. They agreed, although neither thought I would get Jackson to do an interview.

To kick off the tour, there was a press launch on a boat on

Sydney Harbour. I was one of a small group of guests invited to join Michael Jackson on board. I felt privileged to be there, but as I watched the gawking mass of people surrounding the superstar, I doubted I would ever get close enough to him to say hello, let alone interview him.

Then, out of nowhere and without warning, Jackson decided he wanted to pilot the boat himself. People began whispering, looking confused, and a few just stood there, expressionless. A few minutes later, "Captain Jackson" was at the helm and began rocking the boat from side to side, laughing hysterically as people looked on horrified. A few looked as though they might actually throw up. But the more terrified the guests appeared, the harder Michael laughed, his eyes sparkling with mischievous delight.

So this was the unpredictable side of Jackson, playful and childlike, that I'd read so much about. Seeing this at close range made me want to interview him even more.

I asked Gaynor what she thought I should do and she suggested that if I wanted to meet and even interview Jackson, I should first introduce myself to his manager, Frank DiLeo. It wasn't difficult to spot Frank in the crowd; he resembled actor Danny DeVito. As someone with DeVito-like features myself, I figured I'd found an icebreaker.

DiLeo was with Michael trying to coax him away from the boat's wheel. This was my chance to make my move.

"Hi Frank, I'm a short fat British journalist named Rob and desperate to interview Michael," I said, looking him right in the eye.

"Well, I'm a short fat American manager named Frank, so we have something in common," he shot back with his trademark giant cigar protruding from his lips.

"Get Lee Solters to accredit you to travel with us on the tour and we will see how it goes regarding an interview," he said, adding,

"Maybe you can help put out some great press stories for us while we're on the road."

He then gestured for me to come over and meet Michael in front of a giant promotional backdrop for Pepsi, the tour's sponsor.

Michael appeared almost like a porcelain doll as I reached out and shook his delicate hand. His skin was almost translucent, and I swear I could see the inner workings of his veins and arteries through his skin.

He smiled warmly as we shook hands and took a photo together. I remember thinking that the deep Australian tan I'd acquired since my arrival in Sydney made me significantly darker than him—something people always comment on when they see that signed photo of me and Michael from that day.

I told Jackson that I was excited to be joining his entourage on the Aussie tour. He seemed nonplussed; his only comment to me was to compliment the shiny silver suit I was wearing, which I had borrowed from a friend for the event, and is arguably one of the most hideous outfits I have ever worn—and that is saying something.

I went back to the table and told Gaynor the good news, and she seemed even more excited than I was. "Darling, that's amazing," she said. "You can act as our unofficial tour publicist on the road and send me lots of info for press releases while you're with us," she added. It would be a win-win for everyone.

When my tour accreditation arrived the next morning, I was officially the only member of the media traveling as part of Michael Jackson's entourage. I would fly on the same planes as him, stay in the same hotels, and move from place to place in the same blacked-out minivans. In short, I was now a member of the Jackson tour.

There were one hundred and forty-four people on the road with Jackson in Australia, and the equipment alone filled two

Boeing 747 jumbo jets. Among the cast of characters traveling in the crew was Michael's personal celebrity chef and her team of ethereally white-robed women. They looked like human clouds as they wafted from place to place making Michael his favorite healthy dishes. I never got to taste their manna from Jackson heaven, since I was relegated to the reality of eating whatever was served with the band and crew backstage.

One of the more interesting members of his crew was Michael's personal security guard, Miko Brando, son of legendary actor Marlon Brando. He—together with Jackson's longtime friend, father figure, and de facto head of security, Bill Bray—ensured no fans got too close to the superstar. I discovered that Bray, when on tour with Jackson, always slept in an adjoining hotel room or even sometimes the same hotel room.

There was a week of media activities planned in Sydney before we were scheduled to jet off for the first concert in Melbourne. Many of these visits were routine, such as a private tour of the world famous Taronga Zoo on Sydney's North Shore, where the singer happily spent almost an hour among the wildlife. He particularly liked the koalas.

On the third day I got a call from someone on his security team telling me to meet them at the Regent Hotel car park. Jackson was spending the week at Sydney's premiere hotel, which had accommodated all his unique requests including installing a wooden dance floor in his suite. Jackson told me that he used it primarily to wind down and dance off the extra adrenaline after his concerts, which always left him full of energy and unable to sleep.

I met someone from security in the car park and was quickly ushered into a minivan along with Jackson, DiLeo, two security guys and Bill Bray. I had no idea where we were going or why.

Thirty minutes later we arrived at Sydney Children's Hospital and Jackson headed straight for the wards. The kids' eyes lit up as the superstar went from bed to bed presenting them with gifts, CDs, T-shirts, and other merchandise from his tour.

Suddenly, one of the kids asked Michael if he would sign his plaster cast and Jackson began to look around for a pen.

"Here, have mine," I said, handing Michael my dollar disposable pen.

He took it, signed the cast, and continued to sign photos for what seemed forever, but every time we entered a new ward, he would turn to me and say, "I still have your pen."

At first I thought he was just being thoughtful, but by the tenth or twelfth time I was struck with the sense that he appeared more concerned about the security of that cheap pen than anything else.

Finally, I had to say something if for no other reason than to allow Jackson to concentrate on the task at hand. "It's OK, really, you can keep the pen. I have lots," I told an anxious Jackson.

That seemed to do the trick, and he continued handing out gifts to the adoring kids, some terminally ill, until it was time to leave.

DiLeo explained to me that Jackson was adamant that these types of visits not be interpreted as media stunts, and so had restricted it to just myself and a tour photographer in terms of coverage. He went on to tell me that Michael frequently did these kind of secret visits to hospitals and always insisted they were done without fuss and mostly without anyone knowing.

We were almost out the door of the hospital when Jackson tugged at my jacket sleeve. I wondered if I had done something wrong; said something I shouldn't have. Maybe I had annoyed him and he wanted me off the tour.

"Here," he said. "I still have your pen."

At that moment, I could happily have thrown the pen to the floor and stamped on it until it was completely destroyed. However, as I still needed that interview, I just smiled, took the ballpoint, and said, "Thank you. I was looking for that."

Jackson seemed to be warming to me, and I was getting along well with his manager, Frank, who often joked with me, "You're the only one I haven't threatened to fire today."

"Probably because I don't actually work for you," I always replied.

During our first flight together on tour, Frank invited me to sit next to Jackson, which I took as a good sign for my interview. During the flight I noticed Michael was concentrating on a fairly thick book, which looked like an encyclopedia. I asked him what he was reading and he gestured for me to take a look. I was surprised to find that it was indeed an encyclopedia, but a child's version.

I was about to question Jackson about it when he leaned over and said he wanted to share something with me: "Always remember, whatever happens when we arrive at an airport, you must keep walking and look straight ahead. Don't stop, even for a second. If you get left behind, we can't wait for you. We cannot stop moving whatever happens. If we do, I'll be trapped."

I thought he was being a little over dramatic; that is, until it was time for us to exit the terminal building. There must have been five thousand screaming fans waiting for him at the airport in Melbourne, and as the doors opened and we walked out, Australian TV news cameras captured Jackson's smiling, seemingly relaxed face, and me alongside him, my face white as a sheet with an expression of complete terror. My face said it all. It was like nothing I'd ever witnessed. It was a sea of screaming, crying, hysterical fans, pushing, shoving, whose only desire was to touch or even grab their idol or a member of his entourage, which now apparently included me.

I remembered what Jackson had told me on the flight, and so with an open mouth and my heart beating out of my chest, I looked straight ahead and just kept walking as if I was crossing the newly parted Red Sea. The louder the fans screamed, the faster I walked. I must not get left behind was all I was thinking. Finally, we reached the waiting cars, and as we piled in I turned to him and said: "How do you cope with that?"

"It's all I have ever known," he replied.

I spent an incredible ten days with the King of Pop and came to know, if only for a short time, just what it must be like to live in his world twenty-four hours a day. He was unpredictable, introverted, kind, shy, mysterious, playful and, at times, secretive; but most of all, he was a genius. His concerts remain the best live performances I've ever witnessed. I would never be able to reconcile the timid Jackson off stage with the explosive, commanding superstar on stage, who stunned audiences night after night.

And did I get my interview with Michael? Well, not exactly. I never convinced him to sit down for one long interview, but I got more than a dozen short ones that were reproduced by media outlets around the world.

After the Jackson tour and my unofficial role as de-facto tour publicist ended, I decided I needed a change of career. There was no way I saw myself returning to the mundane world of everyday journalism after the excitement of this experience. It was Jackson's publicist, Gaynor Crawford, who first suggested we combine forces and form a new PR company, the Crawford Goldstone Organization, and I jumped at the chance.

She already had a successful roster of clients, mostly handling the PR of international touring artists such as James Taylor, Cyndi Lauper, Tracy Chapman, and Gypsy Kings, as well as many indie folk bands.

Within a couple of months, we had landed some major new projects; the first one having a royal seal of approval. The New South Wales Royal Bicentennial Concert in Sydney would take place in January 1988 at the city's Entertainment Centre. It marked the 200th anniversary of the founding of Australia, and featured some of the country's top performers. The guests of honor were the newly married Prince and Princess of Wales. Although I was excited by the opportunity to work on the show, I was more excited to get a close-up look at Princess Diana.

My chance came backstage at the end of the concert, when the royal couple came to thank the artists who had taken part in the show. I stood behind a pair of female dancers who were anxiously waiting in line to meet them. As Diana approached, she stopped, looked at the nearly invisible spaghetti straps on their costumes, and said with a cheeky twinkle in her eye, "Oh, so that's how your dresses stay up. My husband has been trying to work that out throughout the show." The girls blushed and giggled as the princess made her way along the receiving line. She was definitely not the timid wallflower she had been portrayed as in the press.

The Crawford Goldstone Organization soon landed other major international brands such as the Hard Rock Cafe and Virgin Megastores. The latter meant I was working hand-in-hand with one of the most outlandish, dynamic entrepreneurs in history: Richard Branson.

I looked after Richard during his visits to Australia to launch his Megastores in Sydney and Melbourne. His arrivals gave me a chance to be incredibly creative, as Branson seemed game for anything. On one occasion, I organized for a lookalike of Queen Elizabeth to "knight" him during a mock royal procession to the Melbourne store opening. This took place more than twenty-five years before he would officially become Sir Richard Branson, knighted by the real Queen Elizabeth at Buckingham Palace.

It was during the Virgin Megastore opening at Sydney's Darling Harbour, however, that I was more grateful for my instincts than for my creativity. I had planned a major PR stunt with Branson in which he would abseil from one of the tall buildings onto the tracks of the soon-to-be-open Sydney Monorail, which led to his new Megastore.

Branson was the ultimate fearless showman who loved nothing more than a newsworthy stunt. He was excited for this one, and we had discussed every aspect of the opening. Except one.

A couple of days before the scheduled opening, something just didn't feel right to me with our plan. A little voice kept telling me to double and even triple check one detail that bothered me. I had been advised that the monorail track did not yet have live rails. I wanted a final assurance of this and so made some frantic calls and quickly discovered that the opposite was actually true. It had recently been tested out and was now electrified although not yet in use and, I was to discover, Branson stood a real risk of being electrocuted if he went anywhere near it.

I needed a quick change of plan. After mentioning to Richard that I had just saved his life, I now needed to save the opening event.

Branson would ultimately arrive at the Megastore launch on water skis dressed as an airline pilot and, after doing a few TV interviews, attempt to make an even bigger splash in the press by lifting up one of Australia's best known news presenters, Trisha Goddard, and jokingly threaten to throw her into the harbor to the delight of the cheering crowds.

All these years later, I still keep a personal letter from Richard thanking me for his week of PR in Sydney and gushing, "It was all truly amazing!"

I keep that letter framed next to one from lyricist Tim Rice, who I worked with when I handled press in Sydney for his musical *Chess*, which he wrote with Benny and Björn from ABBA. Their musical features the hit single "One Night in Bangkok," and I recall telling him how it always made me long for the frenetic energy of the Thai capital, where I had spent many holidays.

Little did I realize at the time that I would ultimately come to consider Bangkok a kind of second home, and it would become my safe haven of tranquility for more than six months in 2017, during the height of the RussiaGate frenzy.

Chapter Eleven

London Calling

I had come to Australia on a whim, and I would leave, seven years later, on a whim.

My decision to return to England came about early one morning in October 1991 when I was on business in London. I was there handling PR for the Australian theatrical production of the new show, *Return to the Forbidden Planet,* and had brought a group of Australian journalists to the UK to see it.

It was one of those old-fashioned foggy English mornings I love. I suddenly felt nostalgic for the city and asked myself why I was living thousands of miles away in Australia, when I could just as easily be back in the thick of it in London. Why be nostalgic for what I could actually have?

The time I spent in Sydney was one of the best times of my life. I had made incredible friends, created and run a successful PR company, and enjoyed an enviable lifestyle. And yet I had grown bored.

I knew, on that October morning, that I would not be returning to live in Sydney. I decided there and then not to board the return flight with the group of Aussie journalists, but to make an excuse to stay in London, and live there permanently.

Still, there were a few practical and, more importantly,

personal considerations to take care of. I co-owned an apartment in Sydney's trendy inner suburb of Darlinghurst, and had a company with my business partner, Gaynor Crawford. How would I break the news to her?

I knew that I was making the right decision, but I also knew that telling her would be painful and difficult and one of the hardest things I'd ever have to do. To be honest, I feared the possibility that I might convince myself, out of guilt, to return to Sydney. Telling someone who you love and care about, who has also been your business partner for years, that you're not coming back is almost inconceivably difficult. *How could I do it?* I made the choice, right or wrong, that the only way I could get through it was not to tell her. I would stay in London and not return to Australia. It would be more than seven years before I mustered the courage to call her, apologize, and rekindle our friendship.

Looking back now, it seems insane that not only was I turning my back on my business, my friends and my comfortable life on a whim, but I was doing so without any kind of safety net.

I would leave everything behind, including my apartment; give my belongings and furniture away to friends; and face my future in London with just three thousand dollars to my name. It was insane, but a little voice inside my head was telling me it was the right decision.

I knew that most people would have found the situation daunting, even terrifying, but I found it freeing and empowering. My cushy life in Sydney had given me many benefits, but it had taken away my enthusiasm and drive and sense of adventure.

Whether it was my upbringing or my background as a radio reporter always on a tight deadline, I needed a certain level of pressure to motivate me and fulfill my life. My immediate motivation was to find a job—and fast.

For the next few months, I lived on boxed plain pasta with

canned tomatoes, cookies and cereal. I watched endless daytime TV in a friend's tiny semi-detached East End house, and searched my non-existent "rolodex" contact list for job ideas.

I also reached out to a couple of former clients of mine who were based in the UK. One of them, Stuart McAllister, was the Chairman and CEO of HMV Group, which owned and operated the world's largest music retail stores. I had handled PR for HMV in Australia when they launched in Sydney and Melbourne, and had always got on well with Stuart.

We scheduled a lunch meeting at a hotel restaurant on the outskirts of London's Heathrow Airport. Stuart was constantly traveling and so this was a convenient location for him to meet. I had nothing else to do and welcomed the chance to travel if only as far as the airport perimeter.

I didn't mention my search for work during our friendly two-hour lunch, but towards the end Stuart surprised me by asking if I had already found a job in London. I told him that although I had been looking, nothing had materialized.

"Why don't you work for me as the head of international marketing, bonnie lad?" he asked, using a term that was a throwback to his North East of England background.

"I didn't know you were looking for one," I replied, surprised by this sudden offer of work.

Stuart smiled, took another sip of his beer, and leaned back in his chair. "We aren't, but I think it would be a good job for you and would be a great fit for us."

I said that I would need to think about it and would get back to him in a day or so, but I had already taken the job in my mind. As he would often do in the almost ten years I worked with him, Stuart cut right to the chase, knowing exactly what I was thinking.

"Why don't you decide right now, and we can have a drink to celebrate?"

By the end of the lunch, I was the new International Marketing Manager of the world's largest music retailer. Within a week of receiving my first paycheck, I had moved from East London to the center of swanky South Kensington.

During my time at HMV Group, I would help market and promote their retail stores worldwide including Tokyo, Hong Kong, Toronto, Sydney, and New York.

Stuart appreciated my often over-the-top ideas for both new store launches and creative in-store appearances. I created some stand out ones including appearances by Paul McCartney, Prince, P. Diddy, Mary J. Blige, and Bon Jovi.

I had been living in London about a year when Stuart asked if I was interested in relocating to New York City as part of the company's efforts to ramp up its US expansion plans. He said they could use someone like me in New York. I jumped at the chance, and made the move to a small one bedroom apartment in the West 50s.

I had visited New York City frequently since the age of eighteen. I loved the frenetic insanity and pace of the city, and now it was to be my home, so I was ready to embrace all that it had to offer.

After a few years in my international role, Stuart asked me if I was enjoying living in New York and if I would take on being the Vice President of Marketing for HMV USA. This would mean giving up my international job, but it would be a big promotion as I would have a seat on the executive board of the US company. I accepted the offer, but with more than a few reservations about my suitability for the role and my desire for such a corporate job.

It turned out that I was right to be wary. I was a creative person who worked best when left alone to form partnerships and relationships, and while my approach to my work was unconventional, I usually got great results. This job was about advance planning, budgets, and endless, seemingly meaningless meetings. In truth, I hated every day I worked in the job, and after sticking it out for a year, I knew I needed to quit.

During this time, I had started to experience what I would later learn were anxiety and panic attacks, which manifested in episodes of dizziness, lethargy, nausea, and unsteadiness to the point where I would sometimes have to lean on telephone poles or street signs to keep my balance. I sought the help of a therapist, who attributed much, if not all, of the condition to my unhappiness over my job. I knew it was time to move on. No job was worth living like that.

I told my US boss that I planned to quit, and then called Stuart to let him know I would be leaving. He was an incredibly giving and gracious boss, and it took him just a few minutes to realize I wouldn't budge from my position.

Instead of wishing me well in a new company, he made me an immediate offer: "Why don't you just come back and work for me in your old job? We never filled it when you left anyway, so it's yours if you want it," he said.

It was exactly the reaction I had hoped for and for the next few years I returned to the job I loved, traveling the world, looking at new projects, and expanding the company's global reach.

During my years in this role, Stuart opened the world to me with opportunities and experiences I could never have imagined. On one occasion he invited me to join him at a private reception at Buckingham Palace, where I spent most of the time looking to pocket books of matches or toilet paper with the royal insignia. There were none.

On another occasion, Stuart and I flew on Concorde from New York to London and back again in one day, just to see a concert by our friend, singer Lisa Stansfield. The whole trip took only twenty-four hours, cost thousands of pounds, and although some might have judged it as extravagant and pointless, he thought it was relationship-building and fabulous. It ultimately led to a major promotion between Stansfield and HMV, including her opening one of our flagship stores in Tokyo.

I would stay with HMV Group for over a decade until leaving to form my own New York-based PR company: Oui 2 Entertainment.

Just a couple of years later, I would visit Stuart at his home in Oxfordshire after he had suffered a debilitating stroke. He told me how much he missed his work but believed he was on the mend. A short while later he received another shocking setback; he was diagnosed with incurable lung cancer. He passed away a short time later at just fifty-three years of age.

Bosses and friends like Stuart don't come into your life very often; in fact, I have come to believe that they don't make men like him anymore. His passion for his work and his compassion for his staff separated him from his peers. He liked to have fun and believed having a good time wasn't something to be ashamed of, but to be encouraged and celebrated.

Well, in those ten years, we had more fun than most people could handle in a century. Although he is no longer here, he was one of the first people I thought of when I decided to write a book. I know that if he had been running his company today, he would have made it his priority to secure just about every shop window in his arsenal to help promote it, angering his managers but doing it anyway, just for me, because I was his "bonnie lad" and that's the kind of man he was.

I would experience this same kind of rare kinship only one other time in my career; many years later when I began working with Emin. I remember telling him often how he reminded me of Stuart in so many ways. Our immediate close connection, deep affection, and love of living life to the fullest while having fun, had once again opened an exciting world of possibilities for me that I could never have imagined possible.

Chapter Twelve

The World According to Emin

I have worked with so many clients over a thirty-plus-year career that most have become one big blur. The good and the great, the vile and the not so great who thought they were great—all have become memories of times and places in the history of my life.

Emin, however, was different. From the moment we began working together, we embarked on a road of discovery and insanity and fun where the word "no" did not exist, and where the impossible became just a hurdle to overcome. We traveled the world together, in search of opportunities to propel his singing career to the next level, and we never flinched or backed down from any challenge, no matter how daunting.

Even so, Emin was someone used to getting his own way. In fact, I used to joke that he should manage his career himself, since he was the only one he ever really listened to. When I would say this, he'd laugh and tell me that he did listen to my advice no matter what I thought; and to prove his point he would quote things back to me that I had said and then thank me publicly for my advice and friendship—much to my embarrassment.

Working with Emin was never straightforward but, as his manager, I was always expected to get the job done with the least amount of fuss. He knew very few things could faze me, that no challenge was too difficult for me to attempt to tackle. That ultimately included being the go-between for him and his father with the Trumps. Whether it was a making a happy birthday video starring Trump or arranging the occasional quick meeting between Emin and Trump in New York, I was the one called upon to make it happen. Not surprisingly, when it came to the request for a meeting between the Trump campaign and a Russian attorney, Emin didn't think twice about turning to me to set it up. That was simply part of my unconventional job.

Within weeks of taking over Emin's management, I had put together an international marketing and PR team to handle his music, and we began to travel extensively. We toured Europe, the UK, and even Brazil, where Emin performed at the hugely popular Miss Brazil pageant in Fortaleza, followed by solo concerts and TV appearances in São Paulo and Rio de Janeiro.

He performed to packed audiences in Germany, Ireland, France, and Spain, and even started to gain a loyal following in the US, with sold-out shows in Los Angeles and New York. This was an exciting time for Emin and me. Success in overseas markets was all-important to him—no male Russian singer had ever done it. Emin wanted to be the first.

When I first met Emin, he, unlike the vast majority of Russian artists, sang only in English. It was, I suppose, a throwback to his life growing up in the United States. Emin truly straddled both cultures, having spent his teenage years with American influences, then later returning to his Russian roots. The other major influence for him will always be the culture and traditions of his birthplace, Azerbaijan.

Notable television appearances that helped bring Emin to

a wider American market included *Extra*, Fox, *Entertainment Tonight*, E! and NBC's *Today Show*, where he performed on a live broadcast from the Winter Olympics in Sochi. Once again, his charm and talent won over the audience as well as the hosts, including Matt Lauer and Al Roker, who ended up dancing playfully on screen as Emin sang his new song "Run."

In the UK, I landed Emin a coveted performance spot on ITV's *Good Morning Britain*. Emin performed throughout the two-hour show on a wet Friday morning in London, something unheard of for a virtually unknown artist. Even though we hadn't found that elusive hit overseas, he was still being treated like a star in every country we visited. I knew that we were on to something, and I was determined to do anything I could to keep the momentum going.

I continued to look for opportunities to bring Emin's music to new and wider audiences. In the summer of 2015, we toured Europe with Britain's top-selling boy band Take That, playing sold-out arena shows to thousands of fans. Emin won over thousands of new fans that summer, including the guys from Take That, who quickly fell for his infectious personality and quirky humor.

Another major opportunity for worldwide exposure came in the form of a chance meeting with the head of the Monaco-based World Music Awards. Melissa Corken owned and ran the show that featured performers from around the world, artists mostly unheard of outside their home countries but who were huge stars at home.

She agreed that Emin would be a perfect fit for her next telecast, which would take place in Monte Carlo and broadcast in the US on NBC. We already had a great relationship with the network, having partnered with them on the Miss Universe telecast.

A few months after my initial meeting with Melissa in Manhattan, Emin and I found ourselves in the ultra-exclusive

Monte Carlo Sporting Club rehearsing for the celebrity-filled show. Emin would be in amazing company on stage that night, performing alongside Mariah Carey, Miley Cyrus, Ricky Martin, and FloRida.

Still, the event was not without drama. Some of the performers were late rehearsing while others, including superstar Mariah Carey, took hours and hours of pre-production time, resulting in the show running late by almost five hours. It was such a massive delay that NBC, ultimately, decided there was not sufficient time to edit and broadcast the program as planned. Even so, being part of this star-studded event was another huge boost for Emin, who was presented with his own World Music Award as the most popular singer in Azerbaijan.

Emin is unquestionably Azerbaijan's biggest music star, and his shows in Baku always draw enormous crowds. On one occasion, he brought British superstar Craig David to perform with him in concert on a beachfront stage overlooking the Caspian Sea. The success of this concert led Emin to create an annual music festival there that would go on to become the country's premier music event—"Zhara"—now spanning three days and nights.

Baku is a magical place that I had never even heard of before meeting Emin. He always talked lovingly of his birthplace and encouraged everyone he met to come visit the historic city. He was not wrong about its appeal. Baku is a mix of traditional ancient walled-city charm with a modern bustling center that could easily be part of Dubai or even Paris. Long boulevards and classical architecture sat alongside the limestone walls of Baku's ancient past. The city's central district is flanked by the awe-inspiring Heydar Aliyev Center, designed by the world-renowned architect Zaha Hadid. The building is named in honor of the country's modern day founder, who is also the great-grandfather of Emin's twin sons, Mika and Ali.

Soon, it wasn't just Emin who had adoring fans in Baku. I discovered on one brief visit to the luxury Park Bulvar shopping mall that I had a few of my own. I was coming off an escalator when a bunch of crying girls ran up to me asking for a photo. I asked why they were so upset, and they told me that it was because they knew I was Emin's manager, and therefore "the second most famous person in Baku."

I didn't quite understand their tears, but I posed for photos with them, while making it clear that I was sure I was far down the list of Azerbaijan's VIPs. Inexplicably, this made them cry even harder and they assured me, with teary faces, that I was wrong.

After that, I was quick to mention my new celebrity status to everyone I met in Azerbaijan, including Emin's then-wife Leyla Aliyeva, daughter of the president of Azerbaijan. She giggled at the story, and then with her usual sweetness told me, "I can believe it! You're the second most famous person in Azerbaijan." From that moment on, Emin always joked that I now had my own official fan club in Baku.

Back in the United States, I had the idea of engaging the support of the powerful national broadcaster PBS. I knew they had helped break a number of musical acts, including, most notably, superstar Michael Bublé. I began to develop a live concert project for Emin and reached out to an independent TV producer who worked extensively with PBS. After much negotiation and creative give-and-take, we finally hammered out a deal and came up with the idea of a spectacular open-air live concert in Russia.

I suggested to Emin that we do something in majestic St. Petersburg, ideally in front of the Winter Palace. After tough, seemingly endless negotiations, he and his team managed to get permission for an enormous stage to be built in front of the imposing façade of the stately Hermitage.

In July 2016, almost fifty-thousand fans packed into the square in front of the Winter Palace as PBS filmed this one-of-a-kind concert for broadcast later that year in the US. Emin was joined on stage by music maestro David Foster, who stopped the show halfway through to proclaim on stage to Emin and the crowd, "Remember what I'm about to say to you: America is going to love you."

Foster, a sixteen-time Grammy winner, would go on to produce tracks on Emin's next CD, *Love Is a Deadly Game*, whose title came from a song co-written by me.

Another incredible opportunity for Emin came after I arranged for him to meet hit-maker musician and producer Nile Rodgers. I had met Nile years earlier, and in 2015 he was being honored by a charity I represented. Since my company was producing the charity's gala, I thought it would be the perfect opportunity to introduce Nile to Emin, and I arranged for them to sit next to each other at the dinner. I also arranged for Emin to perform that night. The gala and his performance would be a one-of-a-kind mini-audition, and just as I hoped, Emin, on the night, passed the Nile Rodgers test.

As Emin left the stage, Nile complimented him on one of the songs from his set. It was Emin's new track "Boomerang." Nile told him that it had the qualities of a hit. Emin thanked him, but said it was missing something…Nile Rodgers. A few weeks later, Nile agreed to play on the track and ended up producing it as well. To no one's surprise, the song entered *Billboard*'s dance chart and became Emin's most successful single to date. This time Emin really was on a *Billboard* chart.

After this, Nile and Emin became friends, and Nile joined him and David Foster on stage at a series of concerts in the US, including one at New York's prestigious Lincoln Center. I couldn't have been more pleased. I saw it as another example of my ability to bring people together to make exciting things happen. I had done that all my life and was very good at it. I was able to spot a perfect pairing a mile away and always took advantage of it, often calling in favors to benefit friends and clients.

In fact, it was one of those clients, banking heir turned pop/dance artist, Sir Ivan, who said exactly that in an interview with the *New York Post* shortly after the Trump Tower meeting scandal broke.

"[Rob] does people favors. That's what a good PR person does, introducing people to other people. He knew the sons of two powerful billionaires and he figured he was doing people a favor."

Chapter Thirteen

A Higher Office

Even though he owned a house in New Jersey where his mother and sister lived permanently, Emin didn't spend much time in the United States. In Moscow, he had a nonstop schedule of concerts and promotional appearances, in addition to helping run his family's empire. This meant that when he did travel to the US, the trips were usually short and packed with interviews, recording sessions, appearances, business dinners and, of course, meetings.

On a few of those trips Emin asked me to set up a quick visit to Trump Tower to say hello to "Mr. Trump," as Emin always called him both in public and private.

The first time we visited Trump's office, it was a really windy day, and after shaking our hands Trump gave me a puzzled look, staring at my crazy, wild, windswept hair.

"I hope we're not going to have a hair debate," I said, looking him in the eye. "Because you'll lose!"

Trump grinned and Emin laughed at my bravado. We made small talk for ten or fifteen minutes, thanked him for his time, and then I asked him and Emin to stand together while I took a photo to post on Emin's social media.

The next time we met up with Trump was in March 2014,

when Emin performed at a PGA Golf Tournament at Trump's golf course in Doral, Florida. I had pitched Emin to the organizers of the event, shamelessly dropping our close association with Trump, and they invited Emin to join the event's entertainment performances.

Emin kicked off the night's entertainment, energizing the outdoor crowd, including Trump, his daughter Ivanka, and some of his grandchildren. Although I would later read that Donald Trump Jr. was in the audience that night, I didn't see him.

My first introduction to Don Jr. would happen a short time later, at a dinner hosted by Emin at Nobu 57 in Manhattan. After that, I met him only one other time before the Trump Tower meeting, although I did keep in touch with him via text and email from time to time.

Whether Don Jr. happened to watch Emin perform at the Doral golf event or not, his father certainly did, and he led the crowd in a cheer for Emin. Trump applauded wildly after each song, and stayed until the very end of Emin's performance, congratulating him as he came off stage. Although there were other performers scheduled to play that night, Trump suggested we all head off the course together. With Emin's set finished, Trump was leaving the event.

What happened next was pure Donald Trump. As we were leaving, someone brought over multi-Grammy award-winning music producer and performer Timbaland to meet Trump.

The two shook hands and had a friendly, animated conversation for a few minutes. Trump then walked Timbaland over and introduced him to Emin and me. We spoke briefly before the musician said goodbye. As Timbaland walked away, Trump asked in a hushed voice, "Who was that exactly?"

"Timbaland," Emin said.

"Like, the shoes?" asked Trump.

"No, like the platinum selling music mogul," I replied.

"Never heard of him," Trump said.

Then what had they been talking about all that time? I smiled. It was very possible that at least one person in that conversation had been discussing boots.

The next interaction between Trump and Emin came via a video. I had asked Trump's assistant Rhona Graff if he would record a birthday message for Emin. I expected Trump to video it on a cellphone, but was surprised when he invited me to bring a film crew to Trump Tower to make something more polished. The video was a big surprise when we unveiled it during Emin's 35th birthday party in Moscow, and the more than three hundred guests there that night applauded it enthusiastically.

The next time I was in Trump Tower with Emin, music was again front and center. As we were shown into his impressive office overlooking Central Park, Trump was proudly holding up a platinum disc, the kind record labels present to artists.

He told us it had been given to him because of the success of the song "Donald Trump" (by rapper Mac Miller) and he gushed how the song, which he had been playing loudly, had garnered more than ninety million views on YouTube, which he described as "phenomenal."

As Trump contemplated the ideal place to hang the shiny plaque while playing a bit of the song, I suggested that he might want to take a look at the actual lyrics.

He said the words didn't matter to him; it was the ninety million views that interested him. He seemed to have no interest in the song itself—other than the fact that it was about him and as such had generated enormous public attention and tens of millions of views.

It was on our next visit to his office, in May 2015, however, that Trump dropped a presidential shocker. After fifteen minutes of making small talk, Trump suddenly, almost as a throwaway line, told us of his plan to run for president of the United States.

"Next time you visit the US, I hope I'll be hosting you in the White House," he said to us.

Emin was shocked. "Are you serious, Mr. Trump? You are really going to run for president?"

Trump assured us that, despite rumors in previous years that he would run, this time he was one hundred percent serious and would be making the official announcement in a matter of weeks. Emin and I just looked at each other.

We both shook his hand and wished him good luck, and I went straight into PR mode. I asked them to pose together for a photo with the thumbs up sign knowing that I could post it not only today, but when candidate Trump made his official announcement.

As Emin and I rode the elevator down to the lobby of Trump Tower, we both said the same thing, that we believed he might actually win by sheer bravado, brashness, and self-promotion. As we stepped out onto Fifth Avenue, it suddenly occurred to us that we hadn't even asked Trump which party he would be representing.

I couldn't help but give myself a pat on the back. "So I suppose hooking you up with Trump and the Miss Universe people was a good move, considering you now know the man who could possibly become the next president of the United States."

I figured that if Trump had been able to charm those intimidating Russian financiers and businessmen in Moscow during the Miss Universe visit, he could probably do the same with the American public.

America, in my view, had become obsessed with reality TV, Kardashian-esque soundbites, and constant drama played out in public. So who better to be the reality show president of the USA than Donald J. Trump?

What stood out for me most was Trump's ability to sell himself, to win over and energize people. This was the reason, from the day he announced he was running for president, that I told everyone who asked me—no matter their political persuasion—that I honestly believed he was going to win.

I also enjoyed the reactions I got when anything about Trump came up, or when I referenced him on Facebook. Most of my friends are diehard liberals, so the very mention of his name by me sent them into fits of indignation and fury, and that, for some reason, amused me.

That was the main reason I liked to check in on Facebook on those few occasions I had visited Trump Tower (sometimes I would check in even when I was just walking past Trump Tower). The truth is I'll never lose the naughty schoolboy side of me, which is probably the reason Emin and I got along so well; and perhaps the reason why Trump appeared to like both of us.

But as much as I enjoyed provoking my progressive friends, I didn't support Trump politically. In fact, I've never supported anyone politically. Politics have never interested me. I don't follow them and they're simply off my radar as the more astute readers of my social media understood. Never once, in all my posts, including my posts about Trump, did I ever say or address anything specifically political. It wasn't my world. I've never even voted in an election, either in the UK or the US. While I'm not proud of that fact, it's the truth.

If I had chosen to support anyone in the 2016 presidential race, it would have been Bernie Sanders. A bit like me, he appeared to enjoy being a disruptor, a fearless individual who didn't toe the party line or pay lip service to anyone. He appeared not to conform to anyone's ideas of what he should be, and more than that, he was a one-of-a-kind character. It didn't hurt that he also looked a little like my grandfather, a Polish bagel maker.

Two years later when I testified before the various committees investigating RussiaGate, one of the things I said that surprised them the most was how initially I had encouraged Emin to show support for Hillary Clinton's achievement as the first woman presidential candidate.

Following Secretary Clinton's historic nomination, I helped create a congratulatory Instagram clip for Emin to post using an iconic image of Clinton set to Emin's recently recorded song "Woman." Emin loved it and posted it on all his social media with a caption hailing her groundbreaking achievement. When I looked the next morning, however, I saw that the post was no longer up. When I asked him why, he said he had deleted it because of angry comments from his mostly Russian fans for his perceived support of Clinton, who was hugely unpopular in Russia.

I told the committee members this story to illustrate that I was never pro-Trump nor pro-Clinton. I was always only pro-Emin. My job was to promote him the best way I knew how. Politics was never part of the equation.

Chapter Fourteen

That Infamous Email

The Trump Tower email, as it's become known, was written on the morning of June 3, 2016.

A few minutes earlier, I had received a call from Emin, who asked that I set up a meeting with "the Trumps" in New York City for a "well-connected" Russian attorney who had met with his father earlier that day in Moscow. Emin told me that the attorney had potentially damaging information about questionable funding by Russians to support the Democrats and, by extension, their candidate Hillary Clinton.

The call was very strange because in all the years I had worked with Emin, he had rarely, if ever, spoken about politics. At least not with me. The call was also confusing because of the scant details I was being given. I asked him who the attorney was. He told me the attorney was a current or former prosecutor and, again, used the phrase "well-connected."

"Well-connected. What does that mean?" I asked.

"Well-connected," he repeated.

"Connected to what? The power grid?" I said sarcastically, unable to hide my irritation.

Emin didn't respond.

If I was going to ask the Trumps for a meeting in the middle of a presidential campaign I wanted to know what I was talking about. The last thing I wanted was to find myself being asked questions about this potential meeting without having answers. I didn't want to make a fool of myself, so I continued to press Emin for details, but got nowhere.

Hearing the frustration in my voice, Emin tried to reassure me. He told me that all I had to do was lock in the meeting. I didn't need to attend, coordinate, or report back on it. Just set it up and that was that.

I wondered if he was being vague because he didn't actually know any of the details, or if he was being evasive because he didn't want to share those details with me. Over the years I had come to understand that I could only push Emin so far before he shut down, after which it was pointless to press him further. And that's where we were at that moment. I knew I wasn't going to get anything more out of him.

The truth was, I really didn't care who the Russian attorney was or what was on offer. What I did care about was that I was the one being pressed to make the request. I wanted to avoid a potentially embarrassing situation if someone from the Trump camp asked me to elaborate at any stage, and I was unable to do so because of Emin's reluctance to fill me in. But it seemed that there was no way to avoid or get around that since Emin wouldn't give me any other details.

I knew that asking the Trumps for a meeting with some random Russian attorney, in the middle of their busy campaign, seemed like a big favor to ask.

"You know, nothing good can come of this," I warned Emin, telling him it was a bad idea. I was worried that I was going to end up with egg on my face.

If I was going to ask any favor of the Trumps on Emin's behalf,

I hoped it would be at least something to benefit his music career or his businesses. Not this.

Emin acknowledged my reluctance, but said only that the attorney would be flying to New York from Moscow in a few days, and I needed to make sure there was a meeting in place.

Keeping in mind this was happening long before Russia had become the hot-button topic it is today; so no major alarm bells were going off. The only alarm going off in my head was one of frustration over having to make this request at all.

A year later, at the height of the Trump Tower media storm, it turned out that Emin had apparently felt the same way as I did at the time. Soon after the story broke, he left me a voicemail saying that the request had come via his father, and that he, like me, had also been "against all possibilities of the meeting." I only wish he had shared those reservations with me at the time; I would have looked at the situation very differently.

But that morning, I would do as Emin asked. *The only question was how.* I had two options: write an email to Donald Trump through his assistant Rhona Graff and hope for the best, or send an email directly to Don Jr. who, I believed, was far more likely to respond. Since I still had doubts about what I was offering the Trumps, I chose to send it to Don Jr. That way, I believed I wouldn't make a complete fool of myself with his father should it all turn out to be nonsense.

As I started to type the email onto my iPhone, the paramount thought in my mind was how could I get Don Jr.'s attention.

Although I was worried about embarrassing myself and annoying the Trumps with a pointless favor, by far the worst-case scenario would be if Don Jr. chose to ignore my email. If he did, what would I do then? I couldn't just turn around and go to his father with the same request. If Don Jr. ignored my outreach, Emin and I would not only have embarrassed ourselves, but possibly compromised our connection to the Trumps, which was a valuable relationship for the Agalarovs.

At that point, I was so intent on getting a response from Don Jr. that, honestly, I would have told him I was bringing Snow White and the Seven Dwarfs to the meeting if I thought it would get his immediate attention.

"Good morning. Emin just called and asked me to contact you with something very interesting. The Crown Prosecutor of Russia met with his father Aras this morning..."

I knew I needed to build up the Russian attorney, and since Emin had used the words "well connected" and "prosecutor," I used a term that I was familiar with having grown up in the UK where prosecutors represent the Crown and are therefore known as Crown prosecutors. In the United States, Crown prosecutors are akin to federal prosecutors.

The media and news analysts, however, would lose their collective minds over my choice of words. They assumed, wrongly, that I had used the word "Crown" because I was referring to the prosecutor general of Russia, a man by the name of Yury Chaika. Apart from being incorrect, they were giving me far too much credit. I had no idea who Yury Chaika was, or that his position existed. Aside from that, while there are thousands of Crown prosecutors in the UK, there is only one prosecutor general in Russia. I was using puffed-up language to describe a government attorney and give gravitas.

What I really should have written was that the lawyer was *a* Crown prosecutor, not *the* Crown prosecutor. But it was, after all, part of an email written in just a few minutes, on a cellphone—an email I never could have imagined would be analyzed word by word thousands of times by the entire world's media.

Also, there had been no Russian "Crown" since the assassination of Czar Nicholas and the Romanov royal family during the

Russian Revolution more than a hundred years earlier.

"...offered to provide the Trump Campaign with some official documents and information that would incriminate Hillary and her dealings with Russia..."

No one had actually mentioned any documents, official or otherwise, but I reasoned that since an attorney was the person making the presentation and requesting the meeting, they would undoubtedly have a document or two. And since this lawyer was likely connected to the government, based on what Emin had alluded to, those documents could be called official; in any case, in my mind, documents and official went together like tea and scones. I used the word incriminating, not because I had any knowledge of any law being broken, but because if what Emin claimed was in fact true, then surely this information was indeed incriminating.

"This is obviously very high level and sensitive information..."

At the time I wrote this, I had no idea of the specifics of the information, or if the information existed at all. But since Emin had said that it involved questionable contributions by Russians to the Democrats, and by extension to Hillary Clinton, it seemed reasonable to assume that the information must have some degree of sensitivity. And if the attorney was "well-connected" as I had been told repeatedly, it seemed logical that the information came from a high level source.

"... but is part of Russia and its Government's support for Mr. Trump—helped along by Aras and Emin."

This was pure puffery and even a bit of flattery. But remember, I had witnessed firsthand the reaction Trump had received in Moscow during Miss Universe. It was clear to me that Trump was unquestionably held in very high esteem, not only by Russia's business leaders, but also by the country in general.

Of course, the phrase "its Government's support for Trump" was controversial and provocative, but the reality was that I had no idea if the Kremlin supported Trump's campaign or not. I felt the phrase was justified because I had seen and read much of Vladimir Putin's praise for Donald Trump. As I told the Senate Judiciary Committee, "to me, that is the government, and that is the government mouthing its support for the candidate." In other words, I knew as much about what Vladimir Putin was doing or thinking in relation to the Trump campaign as anyone who read a newspaper or watched TV news. But this, more than anything, is what formed the premise of "government support" in the email.

I would have hoped that people would understand that my email was not an official statement on behalf of anyone, but my own personal opinion. When I wrote that this government support was helped along by Emin and Aras, it goes without saying that Aras and Emin Agalarov do not, at least to my knowledge, help the Russian government in any way. It was pure fawning, flattery by me.

Yes, the email was puffed up and, yes, I tried to fill in the missing gaps where Emin had been vague, but it was what I sincerely believed my client was trying to articulate—and could not or, perhaps, would not.

I ended the one hundred and thirty-seven word email with a very specific question for Don Jr., which was designed to prevent me from having to talk to anyone about any of this and thus prevent my lack of knowledge about who the attorney was or what was being offered from becoming evident.

"What do you think is the best way to handle this information and would you be able to speak to Emin about it directly?"

For me, this was the most important line in the email. I knew that if Don Jr. agreed to this, there would be a phone call between the two of them, and they could no doubt figure it all out between themselves. I could then wash my hands of the entire situation.

I hit the send button on my iPhone.

"Good morning. Emin just called and asked me to contact you with something very interesting. The Crown Prosecutor of Russia met with his father Aras this morning and in their meeting offered to provide the Trump Campaign with some official documents and information that would incriminate Hillary and her dealings with Russia and would be very useful to your father. This is obviously very high level and sensitive information, but is part of Russia and its Government's support for Mr. Trump—helped along by Aras and Emin. What do you think is the best way to handle this information and would you be able to speak to Emin about it directly? I can also send this info to your father via Rhona, but it is ultra sensitive so wanted to send to you first. Best Rob Goldstone."

My email worked. Don Jr. immediately wrote back and agreed to my suggestion, not for a meeting, but that, yes, he and Emin should first speak about this directly.

"Thanks Rob I appreciate that. I am on the road at the moment, but perhaps I just speak to Emin first. Seems we have some time and if it's what you say, I love it—especially later in the summer. Could we do a call first thing when I get back? Best, Don."

I interpreted his response as his polite way of saying he felt he needed a bit more information directly from Emin before he committed to the meeting. In addition, the fact that Don Jr. said "If it's what you say, I love it," was another telling remark. The "if" suggested to me that there was doubt in his mind of the validity of the information being offered which was perfectly fine by me since I wanted to connect them by phone anyway. Don Jr. would later tell the media that he suspected my email pitch had an element of "showmanship" designed to get his attention. It did.

I told Emin straight away that Don Jr. had received my email and wanted to speak with him directly. Emin seemed delighted and immediately agreed to a call. A few days later, I received a follow-up email from Emin asking about the status of that all-important call.

As I hadn't heard back from Don Jr. since the initial outreach, I followed up straightaway with another email to him, believing that Emin was eager to speak to him as soon as possible.

Don Jr. wrote back at once saying that he was free to talk by phone with Emin immediately. This was just the response I had hoped for, but when I tracked down Emin in Moscow, I discovered he was, at that exact moment, performing on stage as part of a concert at the city's Fashion People's Awards. I asked his band manager when he would be available to speak with Don Jr., and was told that he would be free in twenty minutes. I relayed that message to Don Jr., confirmed his cellphone number, and told him that Emin would call him in twenty minutes.

I passed on Don Jr.'s cell number to Emin via email, and since I didn't hear from either one, I assumed the call had gone ahead as scheduled. As Emin had been keen to get this call done quickly, hence his follow-up email to me, I knew that if there had been any problem with the two of them connecting, I would have heard about it.

It seemed all was going ahead as planned, and about thirty minutes later, I received an email from Don Jr. saying simply, "Rob thanks for the help. D." I understood that to mean Don Jr. was thanking me for setting up the call that had just taken place.

I have no idea what Emin and Don Jr. did or did not say to each other on that call—I was never told, but the next day Emin asked me to go ahead and now schedule the meeting for Thursday, June 9th.

"*I believe you are aware of the meeting—and so wondered if 3pm or later on Thursday works for you? I assume it would be at your office,*" I wrote to Don.

When I wrote "I believe you are aware of the meeting," this was to confirm that following his call with Emin, Don Jr. now had all the information he needed.

He responded quickly: *"How about 3 at our offices. Thanks Rob, appreciate your helping set it up. D."*

Three minutes later I fired off a confirmation:

"Perfect...I won't sit in on the meeting, but will bring them at 3pm and introduce you etc. I will send the names of the two people meeting with you for security when I have them later today. best Rob."

All I knew was that it would be the Russian attorney and Ike Kaveladze attending. Emin had assured me that the coordination of the meeting would be handled by Ike. I had worked closely with him during Miss Universe and found him to be smart, savvy, and resourceful. Ike was going to take over the logistics of the meeting since he spoke English as well as Russian. I assumed he would also act as a translator for the attorney during the meeting.

Don Jr. shot back a quick reply to my email. *"Great. It will likely be Paul Manafort (Campaign boss) my brother-in-law, and me."*

This was a surprise. It seemed that Don Jr. was now attaching a significantly higher level of importance to the meeting since the phone call with Emin—enough for him to add two of the most important people in the Trump campaign.

Now, all that was required of me was to meet Ike and the attorney in the lobby of Trump Tower on the afternoon of June 9th to make sure they got through security without any fuss. After that, I would leave them to their meeting and hopefully never hear another word about it again.

Chapter Fifteen

Bait and Switch

On the day of the Trump Tower meeting, I arrived in midtown Manhattan around noon, having scheduled another appointment nearby with Sony/ATV Music Publishing. I had gotten Emin signed to the publishing giant as a songwriter a year or two earlier and was meeting with Danny Strick, the company's US Co-President, to fill him in on Emin's current and upcoming projects. I told Danny about the major PBS TV concert special I had organized that was soon to be filmed in St. Petersburg and would feature sixteen-time Grammy winner David Foster.

I played him some tracks from Emin's new CD, *Love is a Deadly Game*, and teased Danny about the amazing talents of the co-writer of the title track. I said the lyricist was an undiscovered musical genius who he needed to sign immediately. He laughed loudly when I told him that person was, in fact, me.

I had written the English lyrics along with Emin shortly after he recorded the original Russian version of the song. I wasn't interested in a career as a songwriter, but I was over the moon when Emin liked my lyrics and included my name as a co-writer on that track. That was another first for me.

My next meeting was with a friend and client, Barry Dougherty, who headed up communications for the New York Friars Club. During coffee with Barry I kept an eye on the time, between sips of Earl Grey tea, as I wanted to make sure I was at Trump Tower a little early to wait for my visitors. Barry needed to get back to work, so I decided to head over directly and drink another cup of tea, this time at Starbucks on the mezzanine level of Trump Tower.

While I was waiting at Starbucks, I checked myself into Trump Tower on Facebook, a move I was confident would once again send my liberal-leaning friends into a Trump frenzy. This check-in would be brought up to me time and time again during the 2017 RussiaGate hearings. In one of those, with staffers from the Senate Judiciary Committee, I was asked, "Were you keeping the meeting secret?" I replied, "Well, I checked in for it on Facebook, so not really." When asked why I had bothered to check in on Facebook at all, I answered honestly, "Because any time I would check in at Trump Tower, it would annoy 99% of my friends."

Trump Tower appeared busier than usual, with tourists snapping photos, but I also noticed the place was full of twenty-somethings, who, judging by the identical looking ID badges that hung on lanyards around their necks, were Trump campaign interns or volunteers. They all looked curiously similar in their khakis, Brooks Brothers button-down shirts, and overly confident swaggers.

The meeting was set for 3 p.m. But shortly before, Ike called me on my cellphone to tell me that they were running a bit late. This immediately made me tense, as I imagined how easy it might be for Don Jr. to simply cancel the meeting if they didn't get here soon.

I hung up the phone, looked down from the mezzanine and spotted a familiar face in the lobby. It was Keith Schiller, Donald Trump's personal security chief, who I recognized from our time together in Vegas and Moscow. I quickly went over to say hello. He recognized me immediately and we spent a few minutes talking about how things had changed since Trump had entered the presidential race. Keith told me that one big difference was that security, especially for receiving letters or packages at Trump Tower, was now like the TSA's security—the ultra-strict protocol enforced at US airports.

I said goodbye to Keith and paced slowly up and down in the lobby for roughly ten minutes, getting more and more anxious, until I finally spotted Ike coming through the revolving door.

The first thing that struck me was there appeared to be too many people with him. I then remembered receiving an email from the Russian lawyer that morning telling me that she was bringing additional people with her, but now it was looking like a crowd. I had only glanced at the email briefly and replied that she should bring whomever she felt she needed at the meeting. I just told her to make sure they had proper identification. I didn't care one bit who she brought, so long as they weren't held up by the heightened Trump Tower security for not having the correct ID.

What I hadn't done was tell Don Jr. that there would be more people at the meeting. I hadn't wanted to give him any excuse or reason to cancel. But now I was worried that what had been a two-person meeting had become a convention.

Ike introduced the three visitors to me and I shook hands with each person. Having greeted them, I considered my involvement in the meeting to be basically over, so I didn't bother to pay attention to their names—let alone what they did or why they were there. I just wanted the elevator doors to open quickly and send them all on their way to the 25th floor.

But then Ike said, "Rob, since you know Don Jr. pretty well, why don't you come up and introduce us?"

This last-minute request was annoying, but I could see Ike's logic, and at least it would give me a chance to thank Don Jr. in person for agreeing to this meeting. Plus, I wanted to make sure that he was comfortable with these unexpected and unannounced people suddenly showing up.

This new task of making the introductions would take only a few minutes, after which I'd be in an Uber heading back home to New Jersey. My main concern was that between the lawyer coming late and having to make introductions, I wouldn't be able to beat the notoriously bad Lincoln Tunnel rush hour traffic.

We all got into the gold, mirrored elevator and the doors closed. As we neared our floor, Ike told me that one of the men accompanying the Russian attorney would act as the lawyer's translator. I thought this was odd since Ike is fluent in both Russian and English, and I had always assumed that was why he had been asked to attend in the first place.

When we arrived at the 25th floor, the doors opened and we were met by Don Jr.'s assistant. I said hello and we chatted about Australia, where she was from and where I had lived, making small talk about how we missed life down under.

The Russians spent their time taking pictures of the incredible panoramic views of Manhattan and Central Park from the reception area. Admittedly, it is a spectacular vantage point, but I was still surprised to watch this group behave like excited tourists, snapping shot after shot out of the wall of windows.

In a few minutes, Don Jr. appeared and made a beeline for me with an outstretched hand. He patted me on the shoulder and I asked him how the campaign was going. His only response was "incredibly busy." I took that as a subtle hint that time was precious and we were late.

I looked over in Ike's direction and gestured for him and his group to come over and meet Don Jr. so the meeting could begin and, more importantly, I could leave.

After a few pleasantries, Don Jr. invited them into the adjoining boardroom to sit around the enormous polished wood conference table. He was still making small talk with me as they all headed into the room, and while everyone took their seats, I shook his hand, thanked him again for agreeing to the meeting, and told him I was leaving.

Out of nowhere, he suddenly suggested I stay for the meeting, saying it would make it easier to escort the Russian group out at the end. He told me that in any event, it would be a quick meeting, which I thought was perhaps his not so subtle way of making sure these visitors didn't hang around. I told him that was no problem, and took a seat at the conference table, and with that, my hopes of beating the rush hour traffic back to New Jersey were dashed.

On one side of the enormous table sat the Russian group. In the middle was attorney Natalia Veselnitskaya, with Ike on one side of her, her translator Anatoli Samochornov on the other side, and her colleague Rinat Akhmetshin next to him. At the head of the table sat Don Jr., alongside Trump campaign chairman Paul Manafort. I sat next to Don's brother-in-law, Jared Kushner, directly facing the Russian group.

I had not met either Manafort or Kushner before, but both seemed like they didn't want to be there. While Jared fidgeted and kept looking at the floor, Manafort took out his phone and appeared to start checking emails.

I viewed that as a cue that I could also check my phone messages and emails, but I kept an ear open to listen in on what was being said. I wanted to hear for myself just what Emin had failed to explain to me during his original request. I imagined that if anything really shocking came up, while I might not understand the details of this information, I would undoubtedly pick up on an immediate change in everyone's body language.

Don Jr. welcomed the visitors to the meeting and invited them to introduce themselves. He then asked Veselnitskaya to present what she had to say. She had the room's full attention.

The Russian attorney looked to me like something straight out of Central Casting (albeit Soviet Central Casting). She wore a sensible-looking tailored suit and a classic Russian poker face. She also spoke in a monotonous, droning voice and her presentation skills were stiff and stilted, and the combination all but sent me to sleep. I was so bored, in fact, that to this day, I still cannot remember if she used the translator for the entire presentation, or spoke partly in Russian and partly in English.

Almost as soon as she began speaking, I began to look at the latest postings on my Facebook and Instagram accounts. Although I usually consider checking phone messages to be completely off limits and rude during a business meeting, it seemed okay for me to do so as Paul Manafort did not look up once from his cellphone during the entire presentation, except to say hello at the beginning and goodbye when it was over. I couldn't believe how uninterested he appeared in what was being said. On the other hand, I couldn't blame him. I was literally fighting to stay awake as she rambled on.

Given that Emin had said that the lawyer had damaging information, I was waiting for a smoking gun. But her presentation was not only boring but impossible to follow. Where was the so-called incriminating revelation about illicit Russian funding to the Democrats? While I didn't know much about politics, as a publicist it sounded like fluff to me, even if I was only half listening to her.

A few minutes into Veselnitskaya's presentation, I glanced to my left and noticed Jared Kushner appeared to be getting more and more irritated and agitated as she continued with her jumble of disconnected thoughts and ideas. He too began to check his phone and had, as I would later learn from media reports, texted his assistant to "get him out of this meeting as soon as possible."

While I don't recall much of the details of what she said during this part of the meeting, I do remember her making some very general comments about some well-known Russians making questionable donations to the Democratic election campaign. I recall her talking about the Ziff Brothers and about Bill Browder, but at the time neither name meant anything to me. Only later would I learn of their significance.

Jared Kushner's frustration became evident when he suddenly interrupted Veselnitskaya mid-sentence saying that he was unable to follow her presentation and that he had "no idea" of the point she was trying to make. He asked if she could refocus and get to the point "quickly."

To my horror, Veselnitskaya began to repeat the same rambling statement she had just made, starting from the very beginning. This time it was Don Jr. who interjected asking for clarity.

She suddenly changed the subject and out of nowhere began discussing adoption, specifically the ban on the American adoption of Russian children as a result of something she called the Magnitsky Act.

I had no idea what she was talking about. I'd never heard of the Magnitsky Act. I was stunned that this meeting had totally changed course and now appeared to be focused on the issue of adoption, a completely different issue than that of improper campaign funding from Russians, which I had conveyed to Don Jr. on behalf of Emin in order to get the meeting in the first place.

Another thing that was strange was how the attorney's demeanor and tone had changed. Whereas earlier she had been tentative and meandering, now she spoke with passion and authority as she spoke of the Magnitsky Act and its impact on Russian adoptions.

At that moment, it dawned on me that maybe this was a classic bait and switch. Could this have been what the attorney and her team had wanted to discuss with the Trump folks all along? Perhaps the rest of it had just been a ruse to get the meeting in the first place, dangling the idea of illicit funding and Hillary Clinton dirt to get a meeting at Trump Tower.

As the meeting continued, I felt increasingly anxious. After all, I was the one who had written the email to Don Jr. requesting it. I had been afraid of being embarrassed but I never imagined this would transpire.

I shot a quick look at Don Jr. who also seemed perplexed by this new topic, so I sent Ike a short text message, asking what was going on, and why we were now discussing adoption. I suggested that he do something to stop the attorney immediately, as it was obvious to me that it was irritating our hosts. He nodded back to me. I took this as agreement, although nothing changed.

Veselnitskaya's impassioned pitch seemed to go on for an eternity. In reality, it was probably just a few minutes. She then asked Don Jr. if his father could help with the issues she had just addressed. At that point, Don Jr. seemed to have had enough and brought the meeting to an abrupt end:

"I am not sure why you would bring this matter to us. My father is a private citizen, not an elected official. I suggest you would be better off contacting the Obama administration with your concerns as they are the ones who are in power," he said.

I took this as my cue to jump in and thank him for hosting the group. I stood up to show Ike and his party that it was time to leave. All I could think about was getting them and me out of there as quickly as possible. I felt humiliated and I was furious.

Veselnitskaya, however, would remember the end of the meeting differently and tell *Bloomberg News* that Don Jr. had said to her before she left: "Looking ahead, if we come to power, we can return to this issue and think what to do about it," and "I understand our side may have messed up, but it'll take a long time to get to the bottom of it."

My recollection is of Veselnitskaya asking Don Jr. for his father's help, should Trump win the White House, and not Don Jr. offering to help or tacitly apologizing for something that had nothing to do with him or his father.

As far as I was concerned, the meeting was a disaster. It was just what I had been afraid of—an embarrassment and a wasted favor. It occurred to me that this would probably be the last time Don Jr. or Donald Trump, for that matter, would extend the courtesy of a favor to the Agalarovs or ever return one of my emails. It's exactly why I had warned Emin that this whole thing was a bad idea.

As we headed out of the conference room, the Russian group was a few steps ahead of me, and I hung back in order to have a quiet word with Don Jr. The expression on my face was such that he put his arm around me as I launched into an effusive apology for having wasted his time with what I described to him as "inane nonsense."

He brushed it off matter-of-factly, saying that he had been in lots of meetings lately and that these things happen. But he added that he had no idea what the meeting had been about—other than the adoption issue which, he said, they could do nothing about.

A few steps in front of us was Paul Manafort, and in an attempt to try to salvage my own relationship with the Trumps, I brought up something I thought could be perceived as helpful. I asked Don and Manafort if they had seen an email I had forwarded to Rhona Graff on behalf of a friend of mine, Konstantin Sidorkov, a junior marketing manager at VKontakte (VK), the Russian version of Facebook.

Konstantin had asked if I could help him get a social media contact within the Trump campaign because he wanted to set up a page for Trump on VK. I asked Don and Manafort if the best person for Konstantin to send this request to was Dan Scavino, the head of social media for the Trump campaign. Manafort nodded in agreement and Don agreed too, and thanked me for the offer. I told him I would connect Sidorkov with Scavino via email.

I couldn't wait to get out. As the elevator descended, I stood facing the group of Russians in stony silence. Ike seemed to feel my pain and looked uncomfortable and embarrassed. He invited me to join the group for a drink, but did not seem surprised when I declined.

I was fuming and called Emin to vent. In my thirty-plus years of organizing and attending meetings of every conceivable type, this one topped the list of most humiliating. I was angry at myself for not having protested harder when I warned Emin that no good could come from asking for this meeting. I was so incensed that I didn't even bother to check the time in Moscow when I called Emin on his cellphone. It was well after midnight.

"This was the most embarrassing thing you have ever asked me to do. I just sat in on a meeting about adoption," I said angrily, without saying hello.

"Adoption? What are you talking about? What does adoption have to with it?" he replied, seemingly surprised and confused.

I told him the last thing I wanted to do was to relive that meeting and told him to get the details from Ike. Before hanging up on him, and to make my point even stronger, I told Emin that there was no doubt in my mind that this meeting had irreparably damaged the goodwill that had been created between the Agalarovs and the Trumps since the Miss Universe pageant.

I hung up without saying goodbye.

A year later, I would read in the *Boston Globe* how Emin had lamented to Ike about the disastrous meeting. "Just really upset that my dad never listens to me and an amazing relationship that

I've been establishing for a few years with Mr. T has been thrown down the drain."

It has since occurred to me that Emin and Don Jr. have a similar dynamic with their fathers. Aras was called the Trump of Russia because of his prowess as a real estate developer; but the resemblance went beyond that. Aras, like Trump, had a single-mindedness in business and in life. He wanted what he wanted when he wanted it. And both Aras and Trump had adult sons who still, it seemed, sought the approval of their fathers above all else, and followed their wishes loyally, even when it put them in precarious positions.

After leaving Trump Tower that day, I was determined never to speak or think about that fiasco of a meeting ever again. But I was wrong. Shortly after Trump was elected in November 2016, I received an email from Ike asking me, on behalf of Aras, to reach out to the Trump transition team and request another meeting for Veselnitskaya. The email from Ike contained a document for me to forward to the Trump team, outlining details of what Veselnitskaya wanted to discuss. I glanced at it and noticed it was all about the Magnitsky Act.

I was horrified. Although I told Ike I would ask for a meeting, in truth, I did nothing. Over the next few weeks, Ike repeatedly asked me if there was any news about its status. Since I hadn't made the request, I truthfully answered no. This was less a strategy than an act of desperation. The reality was I simply couldn't bring myself even to suggest to the Trump camp that they meet again with Veselnitskaya, who this time was making it clear from the start that she wanted to talk about the Magnitsky Act.

Eventually, after many follow-up emails from Ike, I reluctantly sent a brief email to Rhona requesting the meeting, but I waited until just before Thanksgiving to send it, hoping it would get overlooked or lost in the holiday rush. I never heard back from her. I told Ike that the timing must have been bad.

I thought I had dodged a bullet. But I hadn't. Shockingly, there was a third request from Aras via Ike for a meeting. This one came shortly after Trump was sworn in as president. At that point, however, I was in a position to stand my ground, having quit my job with Emin a month or two before. When Ike told me that "Mr. A" was keen to get another meeting for the Russian attorney, I suggested he tell Aras that it was a bad idea to ask for a meeting since the original one had been awful and embarrassing. Ike agreed and later told me that he had told Aras what I had said, and assured me that there would be no further requests.

How could Aras Agalarov, a highly intelligent and savvy billionaire businessman ask for further meetings after the disastrous first one? The most likely reason, I thought, was that Aras didn't really know how badly the first meeting had gone. I assumed Emin wouldn't tell him all the details and I doubted that Ike had told him the whole truth. After all, no one likes to give the boss bad news.

Strangely, Veselnitskaya would later claim that she had never wanted a meeting with the Trumps in the first place. "I had never been looking for a meeting neither with Trump Jr., nor Sr., nor his team," she wrote to *Fox News*.

She would also tell NBC that she "never had damaging or sensitive information about Hillary Clinton."

In October 2017, however, *The New York Times* would write how Veselnitskaya had arrived at the Trump Tower meeting "hoping to interest top Trump campaign officials in the contents of a memo she believed contained information damaging to the Democratic Party and, by extension, Hillary Clinton."

The same *Times* article detailed how months before the meeting, Veselnitskaya had "discussed the allegations with one of Russia's most powerful officials, the prosecutor general, Yuri Y. Chaika."

This was the same official that the media had (mistakenly) speculated I was referring to when I used the term "Crown prosecutor" in my email. I had actually been referring to Veselnitskaya, but apparently there was, in fact, now a connection to Chaika.

The Times story also referenced Bill Browder and the Ziff Brothers, names I remembered her bringing up at the meeting:

"The memo that Ms. Veselnitskaya brought to the Trump Tower meeting alleged that Ziff Brothers Investments, an American firm, had illegally purchased shares in a Russian company and evaded tens of millions of dollars of Russian taxes. The company was the financial vehicle of three billionaire brothers, two of them major donors to Democratic candidates including Mrs. Clinton. By implication, Ms. Veselnitskaya said, those political contributions were tainted by 'stolen money.'"

And although Veselnitskaya would continue to insist that she was only a private attorney, in an *NBC News* interview in May 2018, she appeared to change her story. "I am a lawyer, and I am an informant," she said. "Since 2013, I have been actively communicating with the office of the Russian prosecutor general."

As the months passed and more details came to light, my puffed-up email would become more and more spot-on. And no one would be more astonished than me. I had hyped my way to helping a client get the meeting he wanted, but now all my hype was turning out to be pretty much true.

Chapter Sixteen

Hiding in Plain Sight

It was the day after the Trump Tower story broke. David and I were still in Athens, holed-up in our hotel suite, and as the scandal continued to get bigger, I knew it was impossible for us to stay. The night before, I was ambushed in the lobby of the hotel by a TV news crew. I spotted them as soon as the elevator doors opened. The young Greek reporter shouted questions at me, while walking backward, her microphone in my face.

"What do you have to say about the Trump Tower meeting?" she called out as we neared the exit.

All I could think of to say was, "The door is about to hit you in the head."

She looked at me, momentarily puzzled, and started to ask another question just as the revolving door pinned her in its frame.

After that, I knew we needed to get out of Athens as quickly as possible. If one news crew had found me, others wouldn't be far behind. And I wasn't hard to locate since I had checked in on Facebook when I arrived at the hotel the first morning. Even if we changed hotels, Athens was too small to stay hidden for long. Someone would recognize me. My face was by now everywhere, on newspapers and TV reports and all over the internet.

But where to go? I had no place to live if I returned to New York. I had sublet my apartment while I went on my gap year. And my tenant had told me there was media lurking in front of the building. The only reasonable option was to return to England.

Although it was 5 a.m., I called British Airways and asked them to book us on the first flight to London. A few hours later, I was there. Ten days earlier I had been in London as a stopping point on my travels. In that short space of time, it seemed my life had completely changed; probably forever, I thought.

As I waited to go through passport control at Heathrow's packed Terminal 5, my first thought was that there might be photographers out front—the ones who are regularly stationed at the airport to snap arriving celebrities and newsworthy faces. At that time, my face was still flashing on news programs and in newspapers around the world, and because I was born in England my story was receiving wall-to-wall coverage in the UK media.

I was about as paranoid as you could get as I walked through the arrivals hall, looking around nervously, ready to spot the first sign of a suspicious glance. I was convinced that every single returning holiday-maker was secretly about to make a call to *The Sun* or *Daily Mail* to tip them off about my arrival.

Had it been a colossal mistake flying into one of the biggest media cities in the world? London had journalists galore. Had I miscalculated? Would I end up barricaded in my hotel room unable to leave? I had nightmarish visions of being the next Julian Assange, who had been hiding out in London's Ecuadorian embassy for what seemed like an eternity.

As I went through the automated passport gates, I breathed a sigh of relief that my British passport wasn't flagged, even though logic told me there was no reason that it would be. To my relief, no one seemed to care in the slightest who I was or what I was doing there. Not one person paid the slightest bit of attention to me. Maybe I wasn't as famous as I thought.

British friends and former media colleagues were sending me links to news stories about me that were appearing ad nauseam, so I decided to take a car into Central London from the airport and avoid the AirTrain, the Heathrow Express, with their live news on giant TV screens in each train. The possibility of my face flashing up on screen and the risk of the ensuing embarrassment with fellow travelers was too much to think about.

I had shared my decision to return to London with a few close friends, who cautioned me to take extra care and perhaps even wear some kind of disguise. The only disguise I should probably avoid, they suggested, was one involving a hat. It seemed almost every picture of me being shown at the time was of me wearing a daft hat. The hats, in fact, had begun to generate their own publicity, including *The New York Times* ("Rob Goldstone, Trump Intermediary, Likes Silly Hats and Facebook") and the *New York Daily News* ("A Brief History of Rob Goldstone's Love of Hats.")

At the hotel, as I was checking in, a friend texted me a link to a story by the *Daily Mail* with the headline: "British PR man at centre of President Trump's RussiaGate scandal fears 'death at the point of a poison-tipped umbrella.'" This was a reference to the 1978 assassination of Bulgarian dissident Georgi Markov, who was walking across Waterloo Bridge when a passerby stuck him with the poisoned tip of an umbrella. The man was a suspected Russian agent and Markov later died.

Ironically, my hotel turned out to be a stone's throw from the main offices of the *Daily Mail*, whose reporters and freelancers had proven relentless in their search for me. One had even flown to Greece after contacting staff from the cruise ship I had been on.

I knew about it because, while still in Athens, I got a text from two cruise crew members who I had become friends with during the week-long trip, and they advised me not to meet them for coffee as planned because a reporter had paid them to pretend he was their friend, and was waiting with them to surprise me and score a photo. I thanked them for the heads-up and suggested they tell the reporter that I had decided to take a last-minute flight to Los Angeles to meet with a lawyer.

Knowing that they might not make much money working on a cruise ship, I told them to make certain, however, that they accepted the reporter's offer of cash. When asked about my behavior on the cruise, I told them they should tell the reporter the truth: that I drank Diet Coke, made silly videos on deck, and usually missed breakfast because I slept late. This pathetically sedate catalog of middle-aged vice was probably not what the freelancer was expecting.

The Daily Beast had run a story a few days earlier that described me as "the playboy who could bring down Trump" and wrote how I hosted "vodka-soaked parties with younger acquaintances at the Russian Tea Room." This, I would realize, was a reference to a birthday dinner for my former assistant, which had been attended by the "anonymous source" for the story. *The Daily Beast*'s description of the people ("largely in their twenties, a lot of expats, all CW-series-regular attractive") and number of guests ("eight") matched the birthday dinner exactly. Needless to say, the guests were friends of my assistant. Buried in the article was the telling line, "Goldstone ended up paying for at least one pricey party at the Russian Tea Room." That was confirmation that the story was written around that one dinner.

Maureen Dowd, of *The New York Times*, then took this caricature of me to the next level when, a few days later, she wrote, "The Trump saga is spectacular, with a dazzling collection of fools and jesters. Who could make up Rob Goldstone, the rotund, vodka-swilling, chocolate-inhaling, British publicist who likes to party at the Russian Tea Room?"

While I'm clearly overweight—I had in fact once written a *New York Times* travel feature titled "The Tricks and Trials of Traveling While Fat"—I'm not exactly sure why Dowd felt the need to ridicule my weight, nor did I understand how it was relevant to the story. I don't drink vodka, and I rarely, if ever, drink alcohol. I certainly don't "inhale" chocolate, not least because I am diabetic. As for "partying" at the Russian Tea Room, I was the restaurant's publicist. Aside from the aforementioned birthday dinner, I was only ever there working, organizing media or charity events.

If I'm ever in a nightclub or late-night venue, it's work-related: working a music gig, producing an event, or organizing a red carpet. That's my job. I never frequent those places except when being paid to do so. It's not that I dislike clubs; I just equate them with work. Most nights, I'm at home drinking PG Tips tea and watching *Shark Tank* or the British soap opera *EastEnders*.

The day after my arrival in London, it appeared that my red herring in Athens had worked. I woke up to the *Daily Mail* headline: "EXCLUSIVE: Terrified British PR executive at center of Russian White House scandal cuts short his luxury European 'gap year' and flees to US to hire a lawyer." I couldn't help but smile.

It was ironic that in my early twenties I had been one of these hungry tabloid hacks desperate to make a name for myself on Fleet Street by getting a scoop at any cost.

Had I not spent every morning for months outside soon-to-be Duchess of York Sarah Ferguson's Lavender Gardens flat in Clapham shouting questions into her intercom about her relationship with Prince Andrew? Yes.

Had I not followed Elton John around Sydney shortly before his wedding to Renata Blauel, trying to uncover any hint that the impending union might be a marriage of convenience for the pop icon, who later came out as gay and married David Furnish? Yes.

And had I not once provoked actress and political activist

Vanessa Redgrave during a rally in London with apparently so many intrusive questions that she felt the need to spit at me? Yes.

I was a working journalist, and would get the job done at any cost. I knew that my editors were relying on me and if I didn't deliver I would be out of a job. That is really the story of my working life. I have always felt I had to deliver.

But never in my days as a journalist had I encountered what I was seeing now. I was flabbergasted at how speculative and downright false so many of the stories were. There seemed to be a casual disregard for accuracy and a total indifference to context in order to feed an insatiable twenty-four-hour news cycle. The need to be *first* appeared to be the chief consideration driving much of the reporting, regardless of how absurd, manipulated or detached from reality the details were.

This experience has led me to believe something I had heard for years, that the term journalist, in many cases, has been watered down to include anyone with a cellphone or bedroom blog who is willing to spend hours sifting through social media posts to create content and headlines. The most disturbing part of this is that respected outlets sometimes pick up and use this false information, and when they do, that false information becomes attributed to or associated with a reputable source.

Many of those reporting my story also seemed frustrated that they couldn't find anyone who actually knew me to say anything negative, or find anything that connected me to politics. The reason for this was because I've never had a connection to politics. So instead, the press resorted to ridicule, parody, and innuendo.

The media called me "flamboyant," "weird," "cartoon-like," "buffoon," "bonkers," "grotesque," "suspicious." There was an endless stream of insults, literally from morning until night, disparaging my intelligence, my business, my appearance, my loyalty—anything and everything that could be faulted and demeaned.

London's *Evening Standard* newspaper wrote, "Goldstone emerges as an unpleasant, wannabe kingpin—the grotesque fool that this drama deserves," while TV host Trevor Noah asked his viewers in reference to me, "Does the Trump family know anybody normal?"

The media universally referred to me as "former tabloid journalist." While it was certainly true that I had freelanced for London tabloids in my twenties, that was more than thirty years ago. My last job as a journalist was in the 1980s with the Australian Associated Press. Yet this fact didn't stop *The New York Times* from featuring me in "Britain's Gift To America: The New Sleazocracy," a story about unethical tabloid tactics and Russian intelligence agency practices.

"According to Mr. Goldstone's account, he moved from local journalism to work for Rupert Murdoch's best-selling British daily newspaper *The Sun* and other tabloids before turning to public relations for pop stars. This career path happens to be ideal training in what Russian intelligence agencies call 'kompromat,' because smear campaigns based on opposition research are a core business strategy of Britain's popular press."

Often, the media were so perplexed by me that they couldn't decide whether I should be feared or ridiculed, so they did both at the same time as one *Business Insider* headline demonstrated: "Rob Goldstone, a man with cringeworthy Facebook videos, could bring down the president's son."

And then there were, of course, the hats. In article after article, and on TV shows around the world, commentators fixated on my so-called hat obsession. Comedy Central's *The Daily Show* ran an entire segment showing me and my crazy hats—fur hats, straw hats, Azeri hats, Russian hats, Greek hats, a fez, and even a gold baseball cap with the word "Cunty" emblazoned on it.

On the occasion of Meghan Markle and Prince Harry's wedding in May 2018, Stephen Colbert, host of CBS's *The Late Show*, felt obligated to point out to his fellow Americans, "When you're watching the royal wedding this weekend and thinking about how classy the British are...I want you to remember Rob Goldstone [as the exception]." A particularly embarrassing montage of my videos and hat photos (taken from my social media naturally) was showcased in the piece.

The funny thing is that I don't wear or own hats. Don't get me wrong; I love nothing better than a silly hat selfie, but I don't actually wear them in my everyday life. But it never occurred to me that my habit of posting endless selfies wearing funny hats would come back to haunt me and be used to mock me.

Initially, when the scandal broke, I had been so caught up in the chaos that a full week passed before I realized that my social media was still open to the public, which is why so many images and videos of me got out. When I finally switched everything to private, several writers then suggested I was trying to hide something.

One of my videos in particular garnered an inordinate amount of attention. It was a video I created about my favorite 1960s UK children's TV show, *Andy Pandy*, which I made on the cruise before we had arrived in Athens. I put on a silly voice, sang the theme song, and marched like a teddy bear soldier around the deck of the ship. I think my parody of Andy Pandy has now possibly been seen more times and by more people than the original black and white BBC TV children's series.

During that cruise, I also shot a few short videos sending up the movie *Titanic*. On the second to last night on the ship, I came up with the not-so-brilliant idea to film the scene where Rose lies naked on a chaise wearing nothing but the famous blue diamond necklace and says to Jack, "I want you to draw me like one of your French girls."

With the help of a "modesty" towel and a plastic blue necklace from the ship's gift shop, I attempted to recreate the scene. It would be my finale video of the cruise. However, after numerous attempts at finding the right angle and endless re-positioning of the towel, I gave up. I decided I couldn't possibly post the video without exposing more than just my humor to the world.

That was arguably my best decision of 2017. Had that video of my bejeweled, naked self been posted, there are no words in the English language to describe what the public reaction would have been. Had that video clip seen the light of day, the last few remaining vestiges of my personal dignity would have gone down like a sinking ship.

Looking back even now, those first few days in London are a blur. I would go down to the hotel lobby each morning for coffee, but really to see if anyone recognized me. The hotel kept free daily newspapers on a stand in front of their coffee bar and so I'd wait until no one was looking, grab all the papers, and throw them in the trash on my way back to my room. I knew it didn't really make a difference, but it made me feel better.

Eventually, I felt it was time that I ventured outside and decided to walk to a café at the end of the street. It was drizzling a little, but it felt good being out of the room. It was only a five-minute walk, just inside the entrance to the Kensington High Street tube station.

I was about to enter when I heard a voice saying something that made my blood run cold: my name. Someone in the distance was definitely calling my name. At first I thought I must be mistaken and ignored it. But the sound grew louder and there was now no mistaking what I was hearing.

"Is that Rob Goldstone?"

The sound was coming closer and I was ready to pretend to be someone else. I speak bits of a few foreign languages, and thought I'd answer in Portuguese or even Thai if necessary. A million thoughts ran through my head, not least how dumb it had been to return to London.

"Rob Goldstone?" said the voice, now directly behind me.

Every muscle in my body tensed up. I turned to face my accuser, but instead discovered a familiar friendly face, someone I knew and liked, and, more importantly, trusted, who worked at Warner Music just down the street from my hotel.

"Jesus, I almost died of shock," I said, hugging her.

We talked for a few minutes about the crazy situation I was in. She kept repeating how she couldn't believe what was going on, and remembered how only recently Emin and I had been in her office playing music and joking around.

After we hugged goodbye and she walked away, it became clear to me that I had to make a decision: would I be a victim, fearing every call and every stare, or would I move forward with my life? Surely, the answer was to take control and reclaim my dignity.

Then, out of the corner of my eye, I spotted a middle-aged man pointing an iPhone in my direction. I decided to postpone my decision to take control of my life and hightailed it back to the hotel.

A few hours later, one of my closest friends, a London journalist and the mother of my Godson, called to check up on me. She reassured me that no matter how dramatic a news story is, most have a life cycle of only ten to fourteen days, after which, she said, the public becomes bored and the media finds a new drama to go after. It was music to my ears, but that still meant I had to lay low for a week or even two.

Frustratingly, the media's interest in my story would last much longer than fourteen days. It would last months and months and well into 2018. The hounding of me, my family, my friends, my clients, and business acquaintances, some of whom I had barely spoken to in decades, continued nonstop.

I was called a "Trumper" and a "traitor." It was suggested my email exposed a direct connection to the Russians and Trump, which could potentially end his presidency.

Some believed I was acting as a de-facto Trump surrogate, while to others I was a possible Democrat plant, put there to demoralize and destabilize the Trump administration. It all depended on what you read, watched, or listened to on any given day.

Conspiracy theories about me raged online. It was suggested that former White House Chief strategist Steve Bannon and I were secretly cousins (I've never met nor spoken to Bannon) and together, we were the new face of white supremacy in the United States. That would be quite an accomplishment for a gay Jew from Manchester, England.

Even comedian Kathy Griffin, who rarely shies away from controversy surrounding Donald Trump, felt the need to delete a photo of the two of us she had tweeted out. She had captioned it, "Don't recall taking this photo with Russian intermediary, but I'm in my 'Dynasty' hat waiting for my interview with Mr. Mueller." I, however, recall exactly when that photo was taken: the night before the Friars Roast of Hollywood director Quentin Tarantino, for which I was the publicist.

And then there was the remark from US diplomat and former ambassador Christopher Hill who referred to me as a "useful idiot," a term attributed to Vladimir Lenin and used to describe unwitting Westerners manipulated for political purposes.

Some media outlets suggested I was sending signals—to the Kremlin or Russia or Trump, I'm not sure which—with my social media posts. One picture of me wearing a souvenir T-shirt of the Russia Winter Olympics spurred the *New York Post* to run the headline: "Man who arranged Trump Jr. Russia meeting posted suspicious photo." They wrote "...Goldstone posted a picture on Instagram shortly after the Nov. 8 election of him wearing a T-shirt emblazoned with the word "RUSSIA.""

In truth, the only reason I posted that picture was because the T-shirt fit me, and also it had a Spanx effect, which was a nice bonus. The fact that it had the word "RUSSIA" on it was, really, beside the point.

The debate of my connection to the Russian government would become particularly heated during an interview by MSNBC host Joy Reid and former CIA analyst, Fred Fleitz, who emphatically argued that any suggestion of my association with the Kremlin was absurd.

"I've got to tell you that someone who is really involved in this intricate Russian intelligence operation would never have sent the email [Goldstone sent]," Fleitz said. To make his point, he held up a picture of me wearing a Miss Universe sash and crown that he had taken from my social media.

Reid, unfazed by the sight of me dressed as a beauty queen, continued to counter Fleitz, who then held up a second picture, this time of me as a pirate, complete with eye-patch and skull-and-crossbones hat. Fleitz eventually finished by dismissing me as "a playboy celebrity publicist who likes to hang out with Tina Turner and Miss America contestants." While it's true that I once met Turner for three minutes, thirty-three years ago, I've never met a Miss America contestant in my life. But what either one of those things had to do with anything, only Fleitz seemed to know.

While it was true that I had no knowledge of the Russian government's involvement, at the same time how could I be sure I hadn't been duped into setting up the meeting? Had I been a patsy? A "useful idiot?"

Although I believed the Trump Tower meeting was a classic bait and switch— the tactic of a lobbyist trying to get her agenda heard by powerful people—how could I completely dismiss the idea that some kind of governmental powers had been in the background of my outreach?

It also appeared I was being thrown under the bus, not just by the media, but by the Agalarovs themselves. These fears deepened when Aras Agalarov was quoted in a Russian radio interview as saying he didn't know me. "I don't know Rob Goldstone at all," he said, according to reports in the UK's *Financial Times*.

Not only had we met countless times, but had flown with him on his private jet, stayed at his Baku estate, attended dozens of Agalarov family gatherings over the past few years and, of course, had been with him in Las Vegas when he first met Donald Trump. I also, of course, had been the one asked by Emin to convince Aras to go ahead and say yes to hosting the Miss Universe pageant in Moscow.

The Guardian newspaper was just one many media outlets who appeared skeptical of Aras's claim: "Moscow insiders said Goldstone was a frequent fixture around the Agalarovs and it was likely Aras knew who he was." The newspaper went on to quote a Moscow source: "I have seen them both at many of the same parties and Goldstone was always hanging around Emin—of course Aras knows him."

Even more than that, on my last visit to Russia, Aras had personally invited me to sit next to him as his special guest along with actor Steven Seagal, at his VIP table during Emin's lavish birthday party.

Interestingly, in July 2018, Seagal was appointed "Special Representative for Russian-US Humanitarian Ties" by the Kremlin. He had become a Russian citizen two years earlier. Seagal was close to the Agalarovs and worked on a number of projects with them, including recording a song with Emin entitled "Boogie Man."

Aras ultimately amended his original statement, and blamed it on a mistranslation. He conceded that he did know me...but "not very well." I am not sure how much more "well" he could have known me based on the history of our interaction and, of course, my relationship with Emin and his family.

The reality of what I knew to be true would also be challenged by the Agalarovs' lawyer. In an interview with CNN's Chris Cuomo, in July 2017, the lawyer suggested that it was unrealistic to think that I would have been asked by the Agalarovs to reach out to Don Jr.

"It's just fantasy world because the reality is if there was something important that Mr. Agalarov wanted to communicate to the Trump campaign, I suspect he could have called Mr. Trump directly as opposed to having his son's pop music publicist be the intermediary," he said.

Of course I had been the intermediary. I had always been the Agalarovs' go-between for anything related to the Trumps. Why would this have been any different? Apart from the fact that Aras barely spoke English, in my experience, billionaires and other important people don't ask these types of favors themselves. They have people like me do it for them. Could their lawyer really not know that?

Cuomo, who seemed to have a more complex understanding of this reality, then questioned him about the phone call I had set up between Don Jr. and Emin before the Trump Tower meeting had been confirmed. The lawyer dismissed the call out of hand. "That call didn't occur," he said. He reiterated his point a short time later. "I'll tell you again that call didn't happen."

This assertion would, in time, be contradicted and proven false.

In a written statement to the Senate Judiciary Committee, some months later, Don Jr. would recall a series of "three very short phone calls" between him and Emin—though Don Jr. couldn't remember what had taken place. "I do not recall speaking to Emin. It is possible that we left each other voicemail messages. I simply do not remember," he stated.

A year later, however, during an interview with HBO's *VICE News*, Emin would drop a bombshell when he confirmed that he and Don Jr. had, in fact, spoken on that call. And he, unlike Don Jr., appeared to remember the conversation in detail:

"I said, 'Listen, there's some people that want to meet you. They obviously want something that could potentially help them resolve things that you could be interested in, or maybe not. If you can spare a few minutes of your time, I'd be grateful. If not, no problem.' Obviously Don Jr., being Don Jr., said, 'Of course. I'll do it if you're asking.'"

Emin's recollection of that conversation was puzzling to me. How could these two highly intelligent men have had a conversation—initiated by my original email—without, apparently, discussing or even mentioning a single word of what I had written? Like so much of what had happened of late, it simply made no sense.

Chapter 17

Meet the Muppet

We spent nearly a week in London, as the press frenzy continued to intensify. During that time we barely left the hotel room. I realized I needed to get out of London and go somewhere to gather my thoughts and figure out my next move. It was time to head east and continue on with my planned gap year. The next stop would be Thailand—as far away as I could get from the story.

Bangkok is a city I know well. I've vacationed there regularly for almost twenty years, and had seen in at least a dozen New Year's celebrations looking down onto the *Chao Praya* river with fireworks lighting up the city sky. Its restaurants and neighborhoods, its alleys and avenues were all comfortingly familiar to me. I even know Bangkok's full Thai name—*Krung Thep Mahanakhon Amon Rattanakosin Mahinthara Ayuthaya Mahadilok Phop Noppharat Ratchathani Burirom Udomratchaniwet Mahasathan Amon Piman Awatan Sathit Sakkathattiya Witsanukam Prasit.*

But I had never spent longer than a month there at any one time, and I hoped living in Thailand full-time would be a real adventure. Within a week, I found an apartment off the always busy Sathorn Road, in an enclave full of expats, cool shops, and dozens of fabulous places to eat. The one downside to being in

Bangkok during the summer months was the heat—it was absolutely stifling day and night. My air conditioning was on twenty-four hours a day for the first three months. Even so, it was wonderful to be in a place where no one seemed to care about US politics, the Trumps, Russia, or, most importantly, me. The main topics of conversation usually centered around the heat, the humidity, and the city's constant grid-locked traffic. It was just what I needed.

Bangkok had always been on my agenda for my sabbatical year. I figured it would provide the perfect backdrop to *Never Mind the Gap,* the name I'd given my would-be book of my gap year adventure. But when we arrived, I realized the narrative of my book would now have to change. My gap year theme would have to wait and my new focus would be trying to figure out how and why my life had been turned upside down by an email.

I began to write and plan my book and enjoyed a peaceful existence for the next four months. It was peaceful not least because I was living under a self-imposed media ban, trying desperately to avoid reading or hearing about the story (even though I, occasionally, would sneak a peek). Friends continued to send me links to articles, and I still received emails with interview requests, but for the vast majority of time my ignorance was my bliss. While the rest of the world was learning the details of the ever-growing RussiaGate scandal as new information came to light, I was frozen in time surrounded by temples and tuk-tuks.

Because of my ties to the US, UK, and Australia, there was a twenty-four hour stream of stories about me going on in the background. When one country went to bed, another was waking up with its own set of theories and conjectures about what had happened, what it meant, and how I fit into the puzzle. The only person who was blissfully unaware of just how extreme most of 2017 had been on me...was me.

In November, I made the decision to sit down for my first

lengthy interview. The writer was British journalist Philip Sherwell and the outlet was the UK's *Sunday Times* magazine. I had thought long and hard before agreeing to the interview, having declined dozens of similar requests. But I agreed to this one because I knew the magazine was planning to devote a decent number of pages to the story, and I hoped that would enable the writer to give the context that I felt had so far been missing.

The interview began one afternoon with some very pointed questions. There was no easing into it. The writer jumped right in, asking about the email, referencing stories and individuals connected to RussiaGate and the meeting; and I immediately realized that I had no idea what he was talking about. Fusion GPS? No idea. The Magnitsky Act? A little. The Steele dossier? Even less.

I didn't know what to do or how to answer, or why I had agreed to the interview in the first place. Even stranger, only then did it hit me: I had never read the entire Don Jr. email chain, even though it had been in the news almost every day since first being published. I had written those emails, but I wasn't familiar with them, and barely remembered what was in them. I was almost as clueless now as I had been when I wrote that first email.

Conducted over two days, the interview was the wake-up call I needed. As I faced question after question about things I'd shut out of my mind to get through the ordeal, I knew I could no longer live in the dark. After the final session was over, I went online and began to read the hundreds of articles, tweets, blogs, and theories about me, my emails, the Trump Tower meeting, and anything else I could find. I let in all the things I'd blocked out the moment I left London.

This was the right move on my part because I was only weeks away from what would become a true test of my stamina and memory. I only had a few months left of my gap year in Bangkok when I arranged to fly back to the US in December 2017 to meet with the official bodies investigating RussiaGate: the Senate Judiciary Committee and Senate and House Intelligence Committees. They had reached out asking if I would attend voluntary interviews as well as submit relevant emails, texts, voicemails, and other information relating both to the Trump Tower meeting and the Miss Universe pageant. They wanted to discuss these issues, and no doubt much more, in person with me in Washington DC.

I was keen to tell my side of the story to the officials doing the investigating, and had made it clear from day one that I would always be available in a voluntary capacity. There was no reason, I felt, to postpone any of the hearings, other than the logistical issue of my currently living thousands of miles away in South East Asia.

Some commentators had speculated that it was strange, or perhaps "convenient," that I had gone overseas right when the story had broken. In fact, a reporter from *The New York Times* had suggested to me that my timing might have been influenced by these events. But that was simply untrue, and I asked the reporter one simple question: "If your newspaper broke the story from an anonymous tip, how could I possibly have known beforehand?" I added that my gap year had been planned and discussed with friends more than a year in advance, something the UK's *Sunday Times* journalist confirmed independently and corroborated in his feature story.

She seemed to agree, but then asked me how I could afford to take a year off, lamenting that she wished she could do the same. I had worked since I was sixteen years old, never attended university, and never had the chance to take a student gap year. I had dreamed about taking this time off for myself for decades, and now was finally doing it. In the end, I told the writer that it *would probably do her some good* to take a gap year herself.

My plan was to return to New York in early 2018. That would be the official end of my time away. I had hoped I could schedule the Washington DC interviews after my return, but it seemed they preferred to have me come in earlier.

So I decided to fly to New York a day or two after my birthday in December, meet with my attorneys, travel to Washington to testify, and then go back to Thailand for a final few weeks of peace and quiet. I knew it would be a long, exhausting 17,000-mile round trip, but I also thought that once I had testified, it would hopefully mark the beginning of the end to this traumatic chapter in my life.

Two days before I was to fly to Washington, on the morning of my birthday, I received an unexpected text message. It was from Emin. He wished me well, adding his hope for "All the clouds to pass and sunshine always be above."

At first, I ignored his message and thought I wouldn't reply. There were so many things I wanted to say to him. I wanted to shout at him and ask why he had allowed me to be put in this horrific situation. Why had he not shared his own misgivings and concerns about this meeting at the time of our first call? If he had, I was sure I could have forced him to convince his father it was a bad idea.

But in the end, I just took a deep breath and answered his message simply: "All I can do is somehow hope for the best."

Within seconds, Emin replied: "All will be fine!!! Stay well!!! Thinking of you!!!"

The following day, just twenty-four hours before I would board the flight to the US, I received a series of media calls saying there was a new development in the story. It appeared sources had described an email I had written to Emin and Ike a few days after the Trump Tower meeting, detailing me having seen a story about Russians possibly hacking DNC emails. I had seen it on CNN, in my hotel room, during a brief visit to Montreal. I sent an email about this breaking story to Emin and Ike, and added the words "eerily weird."

I had written those words because the report appeared to involve two things that rang a bell with me: Russians and the DNC. I thought it "eerily weird" because only days earlier, I had been in that Trump Tower meeting, which was also supposedly about Russians and the DNC, yet had turned out to be about adoption.

Now, a year and a half later, it appeared that email was being made public, and CNN was running a news report about my reaction to their news report. In other words, CNN was reporting on me "reporting" on them. It was surreal.

The media was also reporting on another new development that involved me. This one concerned VKontakte (VK), Russia's version of Facebook. The report centered around the email I had forwarded from Konstantin Sidorkov, my friend who worked at VK, and who wanted to invite Donald Trump to open his own page on the hugely popular social media network. He had asked me a number of times if I could connect him with a social media contact in the Trump campaign.

I had first met Konstantin Sidorkov in 2013, at Emin's press conference in Moscow to launch the video for his single "Amor," which featured Olivia Culpo. The press conference took place at Emin's newly opened Rose Bar, which was perched above Nobu restaurant in the center of the city. The bar and restaurant were designed to resemble the inside of a luxury yacht and even had a retracting roof, something you don't see every day in Moscow, with its seven months a year of wintery weather.

Emin had suggested that I join him and Olivia on the makeshift dais to talk to the media about the video. He said this would also give him an opportunity to introduce me to the Russian media as his new manager. As we took our seats on the sofas, I looked out at a sea of reporters, most of whom had come to see the world's most beautiful woman. The most eager appeared to be two young radio reporters in the front row.

From their microphone flag, I could see they worked for NRJ Radio, a huge pop music station in Russia. They looked as if they were still in high school. One of them in particular resembled a Muppet: a frenzy of crazy, curly blond hair, giant blue eyes, and a round, pudgy face.

Throughout the press conference, the Muppet never took his eyes off Olivia and when the event was over he bolted over to me, introduced himself and his colleague, and begged for a photo.

"With me?" I joked.

"No, not you. With Olivia. She's the most beautiful woman I've ever seen," he said in almost perfect English.

"Sure, I can arrange that." I gestured for him and his friend to follow me to where Olivia was standing, surrounded by journalists.

"By the way, are you old enough to work? You look like you're twelve years old," I joked.

He assured me that not only was he old enough to work, but also to drink, as he grabbed a beer.

"I have someone I want you to meet," I told Olivia. "It's a Muppet," I blurted out (chiefly because I hadn't remembered to ask his name).

Olivia laughed and posed with him for picture after picture, which would adorn not just his radio station, but his social media feed for days.

I took my own photos and captioned them with the word "Muppet," a term that stuck to him so much that he would end up calling himself The Muppet. It led to me tagging other Muppet-looking people I met around the world, much to the amusement of my friends on Facebook.

The Muppet would often invite me to concerts and events when I was visiting Moscow. Selfishly, I knew that it could only help Emin's career for me to be friendly with a Russian radio guy, but at the same time, he was great fun, spoke very good English, and knew a totally different group of cool, fun people than Emin's usual crowd.

After leaving his radio job and joining VK's marketing and promotions department, Sidorkov believed it would be a good career move for him to convince Donald Trump to open a social media page on VK. He knew that I had met Trump and worked with him on Miss Universe, so it was natural that he would reach out to me for help.

At first, I ignored his requests to hook him up with someone at the Trump campaign who handled social media, but eventually I gave in and sent a note to Rhona Graff asking her for someone he could contact. She suggested Dan Scavino, the campaign's head of social media, and I passed that name to Sidorkov.

I had also taken the opportunity at the end of the Trump Tower meeting, as we walked out of the boardroom, to ask Don Jr. and Paul Manafort if Scavino was indeed the right person to send the VK request to. They had both agreed he was.

I had passed on this information to Sidorkov in an email, and it was *this* email that was now making headlines. In reality, no one ever took the twenty-year-old up on his offer; the page was never created, and I never gave it another thought. That is, until I saw it on CNN.

The fact that Sidorkov had a connection to me and worked for VK was enough to raise eyebrows and make him part of the RussiaGate story. His outreach to Trump through me was now falsely being linked to reports of America's Facebook being invaded by government-sponsored Russian internet trolls trying to influence the election in a series of excited headlines.

"Russian social media giant offered pro-Trump effort during campaign" (ABC); "Russian social media executive sought to help Trump campaign in 2016, emails show" (*The Washington Post*); "Exclusive: Previously undisclosed emails show follow-up after Trump Tower meeting" (CNN); "Russian social media exec reached out to Scavino, Trump Jr. during campaign: report" (*The Hill*).

The less than exciting truth was that American Facebook has nothing to do with VK, and I have absolutely nothing to do with either one—other than having my own personal Facebook account. But I did have a friend who worked at VK, and he did want to score a big celebrity "get" like Donald Trump and create a social media page for him since that was his job. As a friend of Sidorkov, and someone who had also started working as a journalist at sixteen, all I had done was try to help him forward his request to the right individual. That was all.

Sadly, the episode only reaffirmed my somewhat cynical mantra: "No good deed goes unpunished." I had tried to help a friend, and it had blown up in my face.

It seemed that even a Muppet wasn't immune from guilt by association in this on-going saga.

Chapter 18

Capital Punishment

I landed at New York JFK airport's packed Terminal 4 early on the afternoon of Sunday, December 9, 2017. As I exited the terminal building, I was greeted by a snow storm. It seemed surreal that just twenty-four hours before I had been wearing shorts and flip flops in the scorching heat of Bangkok, and now I was freezing despite wearing a quilted jacket, a thick sweater, and two scarves.

Heading into Manhattan by Uber, I had no idea how the next week would play out. I had decided to stay at the Hudson Hotel, mainly because it was conveniently situated near my attorney's office and just steps from Central Park. One thing I had failed to remember when booking it was that the hotel was almost directly opposite the studios of CNN, who had been relentless in trying to get me to sit down for an interview. I decided I would definitely be wearing my new "disguise" of black-rimmed glasses and a hoodie whenever I ventured past their Time Warner Building offices.

I was now in New York as a tourist rather than as a resident and it felt odd. That first night, I couldn't sleep due to jet-lag, the newness of my surroundings, a sizable dose of anxiety, and the intimidating prospect of testifying before Congress. I woke up

early and, although it was still freezing, decided to visit a familiar, comforting breakfast haunt. It was only a ten-minute taxi ride
to one of my favorite eateries, Barney Greengrass, a Jewish deli
and restaurant on the Upper West Side. When I first moved to
New York from England I used to go there every Sunday, since the
Jewish food reminded me of my childhood.

Usually the place was packed. But this morning there were
plenty of free tables, and I spied a small one in the back. As I
headed over, I noticed a familiar face. Allen Grubman was one of
America's best known entertainment attorneys, and I had known
him for many years as we shared a handful of mutual friends.

"Aren't you in jail?" screamed a smiling, red-faced Grubman
from across the room.

He laughed out loud and gestured for me to come sit with him
and his guest. I declined with a smile, preferring to sit alone with
my thoughts and my bagel and lox. As I was leaving, however, he
gestured once again for me to come over, and this time I took a
seat at his table.

He asked me how I was and what I was doing back in the US,
and I told him I was headed to Washington to meet with the various committees. He nodded and said, "I have known you a long
time, and just want to give you one piece of free advice. No matter what you do, when they ask you questions, just tell the truth.
Don't lie. That's how they get everyone."

I thanked him, assured him I had no plans of doing otherwise, and left the restaurant for a meeting with my attorneys. I
had to get ready for a grueling schedule of three eight-hour days
of intense back-to-back interviews in DC. Because I would only
be in the US a short time, I would have to squeeze in all the interviews before I returned to Thailand.

The first of the hearings would be with staffers from the Senate
Intelligence Committee, my first taste of giving testimony to

anyone, anywhere, let alone to representatives of the US government. It was a scary thought.

The following day would be a repeat performance but with staffers representing the Senate Judiciary Committee. Even the word judiciary had a frightening ring to it. I was not looking forward to it.

A couple of days after that I was scheduled to appear in a closed session before members of the House Intelligence Committee. This interview would take place inside the Capitol building and it would be with members of Congress. Another terrifying thought.

I had been told there really was no way to appreciate the intensity of being a witness in this kind of political investigation. No matter how prepared I was, I knew I was going in blind. This was clearly uncharted territory for me.

On the Amtrak Acela train from New York to Washington, I could think of little else except what lay ahead: Would I be able to handle the questions without either going blank or remembering something incorrectly? Would I be able to get my points across clearly? Would they see how my job as a publicist and manager had landed me in this situation in the first place? Would they understand that I was a bit player in this drama?

Those were the questions that were going round and round in my mind as the express train hurtled down the northeastern corridor toward the nation's capital.

One thing I did know, and I had known it from the very beginning: I simply had to tell my story. Tell the truth. I didn't care if it pleased one side, both sides, or no sides at all. I didn't care if it embarrassed me or made me look like a naive fool.

What was important to me was only that I give the most accurate recollection that I could. The rest would be up to the people handling the investigations.

I checked into the Hyatt Regency on Capitol Hill, and went for dinner with two friends who happened to be in Washington that night. I was surprised to learn that one of them had testified to a congressional committee during the Clinton controversy surrounding Monica Lewinsky. He said, based on his experience, he could offer me two important pieces of advice: "Make sure you don't unwittingly say something that isn't true," and "Wear a tie."

Of course I was going to tell the truth. But, I told him, I rarely if ever wore a tie and, to be honest, ties made me uncomfortable.

"Good," he said. "You're supposed to be uncomfortable when testifying. Make sure you wear one."

On the first day I was to testify, I got up extra early and took a walk in the freezing morning air to clear my mind. It was in the low twenties, but felt even icier as I had been in the high nineties for the past half year. Maybe because I'm English, I felt reassured and almost comforted by the cold weather.

My two attorneys arrived at the hotel lobby around 8 a.m., and we decided to walk to the interview. I was wearing a suit that had been custom made for me in Bangkok for the occasion, since nothing would fit me off the peg and my other suits were packed away with my apartment furniture. Fortunately, I had packed a tie and put it on, after deciding my friend had been one hundred percent correct. I was now suitably uncomfortable and ready to testify.

It was already snowing and there was a kind of charm to how the city looked as we approached the nondescript modern Senate office building. The plain utilitarian facade seemed almost out of place sitting opposite the imposing classical grandeur of the Capitol and its dome.

Given how contentious and controversial the subject was, I knew I had to approach this hearing as if every word I spoke could be twisted, turned, examined, attacked, dismissed, debated, and ultimately used as a weapon against me. Each word and description I uttered needed to be accurate and to the point. I knew I had to try and avoid my urge to speculate and, more importantly, attempt to suppress some of my favorite adjectives such as ludicrous, vile, useless, ridiculous, and divine. For the past six months I had been accused of being over-the-top, prone to exaggeration, hyperbolic, and tabloid. I wanted to make sure my testimony and the language I used today was different from that of my everyday PR life for the same reason I was wearing a suit and a tie.

After passing through security, we were shown into the interview room, which quickly filled with staffers of both the majority (Republicans) and minority (Democrats). They would be my inquisitors today and, judging by the sheer number of them, it was going to be a long day.

Once I sat down, the questions came fast and furious, delivered randomly by whomever seemed to get in first. There didn't appear to be any kind of pecking order. I hadn't realized how divisive and partisan these hearings would be. I suppose I should have known it would be like that, but my attention had been on what I would say.

One positive aspect was that this would be the first time I was able to tell my complete story from beginning to end to people whose decision-making could potentially be influenced by what I had to say. If it helped clear up some of the misreporting and mischaracterizations, then I was happy to be there.

Throughout the day, I was shown dozens, perhaps even hundreds, of documents, emails and text messages, and asked searching questions about them. Many of these items I had already produced as I had either written or received them, while some had been produced in advance by others who had testified earlier, so this was the first time I was seeing them. I carefully answered questions about each one's relevance, context, and meaning, trying my best to stay focused and on point, yet give a complete picture of events.

Despite my best efforts, on a few occasions my irreverent side came out in my answers; fortunately, it seemed to bring a few moments of much appreciated and certainly much needed levity to the room. At one point I was asked whether there had been any important Russians at the dinner in Las Vegas that Emin and I had attended with Donald Trump. I had already answered the question to the best of my ability, and couldn't help blurting out that "Obviously, Vladimir Putin had been sitting on my lap [during the dinner]."

My off-the-cuff remark brought a momentary smile to the faces in the room, but not before my attorney quickly pointed out emphatically, for the record, that his client had, of course, been making a joke. I was now in a world where someone might publish a story with the headline that read: "Putin in British Publicist's Lap During Vegas Dinner."

Keeping my irreverence in check, suppressing my tendency to speculate, and resisting the impulse to entertain for eight straight hours was exhausting. I eventually finished my testimony and realized, with horror, that I would have to do the same thing all over again the next day.

The next interview was with staffers from the Senate Judiciary Committee. I doubted that it would be easier than the day before, despite being told that having done it once, it would at least seem easier. It wasn't just the exhausting nonstop barrage of questions that made testifying so difficult; it was having to recall specific dates, incidents, and dialog that went back years that became taxing as the day went on.

Just try to remember what you said to your friends a week ago. Then try to imagine repeating it almost word for word to a room of strangers, some of whom have a very specific idea of how your testimony should sound to make their point stronger.

As we all took our seats, I couldn't help but notice that the lead counsel for Senator Dianne Feinstein reminded me of British actress, Dame Judi Dench. In the end, it turned out that Dame Judi's lookalike was just as intimidating in her questioning of me as Dame Judi is when addressing James Bond on screen. At any moment I expected her to scold me with the words, "Oh, grow up 007."

This second day would follow a more regimented format. There would be a strict one hour of questioning by staffers representing the Republicans, followed by an hour from the Democrats. The process would be easier to understand, but it would be another full day of being asked what seemed like the same questions over and over again, and then having those questions repeated in a slightly different way by the other side.

I tried to explain as best I could how, without context, people might find it hard to understand why I wrote or said things the way I did. A throwaway line can appear to have limitless under-lying or hidden meanings when viewed out of context or when twisted and manipulated to fit a particular narrative, storyline or political agenda.

That is what I fought hardest to make everyone understand throughout the hearings; that my role couldn't be understood without context.

Months later I met up with a friend in the media who told me something that resonated deeply. "The problem we have in the media is that everyone who has context doesn't want to talk to us, and everyone who wants to talk doesn't have context," he said. It's what I had been saying for almost a year. The talking heads and news commentators appeared to know what they were talking about. But I knew the facts and it was excruciating watching them hypothesize and many times just make things up.

One thing I particularly wanted to emphasize in the judiciary hearing was how against the Trump Tower meeting I had been. I explained to them that I had cautioned Emin on that first phone call that no good could possibly come of this request; neither he nor I knew anything about politics, he couldn't articulate what I needed to know about this planned meeting, and it was a waste of a major favor from the Trumps.

When the Senate Judiciary Committee finally released the transcripts of its interviews in May 2018 this fact was, thank goodness, picked up by most of the mainstream media.

However, other inaccurate stories continued to be reported. One such example was an online report by CNBC that said there was a "newly revealed connection" between me and then White House communications director Anthony Scaramucci. I had received an email from someone claiming to be Scaramucci, but I thought it was a fake, passed it onto my attorneys, and told the committee all of this. The testimony appeared in the published transcript.

CNBC claimed, however, that according to an unnamed source, Scaramucci considered me "a good guy" and had met me "a few times" before he wrote that email to me. This was categorically untrue.

The CNBC report went on to claim that their source "declined to explain the substance of Scaramucci's meetings with Goldstone," but when asked why he had "interacted" with me, they stated "Goldstone was helpful on the campaign." When asked to explain further how I was "helpful," the source's answer was vague but said that I was "just hanging around the campaign. Nothing specific."

CNBC reported that it had asked Scaramucci to comment, but he had "declined." I was never called for comment. The story got an enormous amount of pick up. It was not only entirely false, but it could easily have been checked by reading the relevant part of the committee transcript.

I found the episode incredibly frustrating. The writer appeared to use the hearing transcript from the Senate Judiciary Committee as the basis for the story. He wrote, "The email in question, sent days after Trump appointed Scaramucci as White House communications director, was buried among more than twenty-five hundred pages of documents pertaining to the June 2016 meeting," but then ignored my very clear answers in the exact area of the transcript that was being referenced. He appeared simply to skip over it. My answers made it clear that the Scaramucci email, as far as I knew, was fake and that I had paid no attention to it. I had never had any interaction with Scaramucci. As for the writer's assertion through this "unnamed source" that I had been "helpful" and often been seen "just hanging around the [Trump] campaign," again this was one hundred percent false.

When the first two interviews were over, I decided to stay in DC over the weekend rather than go back to New York since I needed to return on Monday to face what I imagined would be the most daunting of the three committees—the House Intelligence Committee. At this next hearing, I would no longer be interviewed by staffers, but would take questions directly from members of the US Congress.

I woke up early on Saturday morning, put on a pair of sweatpants and a hoodie, and headed to Georgetown, my favorite part of DC. Years earlier, while working for HMV, I had helped open their record store in Georgetown and remembered how much I enjoyed its village feel and lively atmosphere.

The streets were already starting to get busy with weekend shoppers, and I spied a coffee shop and headed there for a break. I was standing on the crosswalk, waiting for the lights to change, when I noticed a woman pointing her cellphone at me. Although she was carrying shopping bags in one hand, it was obvious to me that she was taking a video or photo of me.

So far my trip to DC had pretty much gone under the radar

and the media had only caught a brief glimpse of me entering one of the committee rooms. The last thing I wanted now on my day off was for someone to snap and then post or sell a photo of me looking exhausted, disheveled, and in badly fitting sweats. But there was nothing I could really do but get off the street and hope I was being paranoid.

Two hours later, a friend of mine called from New York to say he had just seen an unflattering photo of me crossing the street in Washington posted online. My instinct had been correct; the woman apparently had sold this image of me to a national photo agency. So after avoiding photographers around Capitol Hill all week, I had finally been snapped by a Saturday morning shopper with an cellphone and an eagle eye.

As a result of this, I spent the rest of the weekend mostly in and around my hotel. I was counting down the days until I could jet out of Washington and return to the cocoon that I inhabited in Bangkok. But before I could even think of warmer climes, there was still the all-important hearing with members of Congress.

By 9 a.m. Monday morning I was walking with my attorneys toward the steps of the imposing Capitol building, ready to be questioned by members of the House Intelligence Committee.

Having never visited the Capitol building as a tourist, my interrogation would be my first experience inside this bastion of American politics. I walked through the vast public foyers, mingling with visitors from around the globe all looking wide-eyed at this chamber of American power. I was jealous of those tourists. They were there to gaze in awe at a piece of American political history; I, on the other hand, was about to become a small part of American political history.

This time, the people asking the questions would be actual politicians who, no doubt, would have their own agendas and partisan ideas.

Once I entered the hearing room, I was quickly faced with a dozen or more congressmen. Among the questioners for the Republican majority was South Carolina Congressman Trey Gowdy, a slight man with a shock of steel gray, slicked-back hair, whose look and demeanor made me think immediately of a whippet, while opposite him and leading the questioning for the Democrats was California Congressman Adam Schiff, who at times during the day reminded me of a kind of angry schoolboy seemingly ready to stamp his feet in protest if he didn't get the answers he wanted.

Most of my time in the hearing was spent answering questions put by Schiff. That made sense, as it was the Democrats who were looking for answers, while the Republicans seemed to be trying to prove that there was nothing to answer. The committee, in other words, was intensely political, so much so that some of the congressmen had trouble even conceiving of the possibility that a person like me might not have a political bias.

Congressman Gowdy, in particular, seemed utterly perplexed by the story I related to the committee about my having encouraged Emin to post a short video I created to celebrate Hillary Clinton's milestone nomination, using one of his newly recorded songs "Woman." The words of the song and its message seemed a perfect fit for Clinton's achievement in being the country's first female presidential candidate, especially the chorus which begins:

"No matter what they say about you, woman, I know you're amazing…"

I told the committee that Emin had loved my idea and I quickly put together a short video clip for him to post on his social media. Within minutes of finishing it, he had posted it on his official Instagram page. We then discussed the possibility of perhaps sending the song to the Clinton campaign in the hope they might possibly use it during her run.

I explained to them how the next morning the social media post had disappeared. Emin told me he had decided to take it down after an outpouring of negative comments online from his mostly Russian fans who were angry at his apparent support for Clinton, who was unpopular in Russia.

I brought up this story at the hearing in order to show members of the committee that I was neither pro-Trump nor pro-Hillary. I was pro-Emin. I was constantly looking for new and interesting ways to associate Emin with global events and opportunities to expand his musical reach and find new audiences.

This story, however, seemed to baffle Congressman Gowdy, who repeatedly asked me to explain why it was that we had supported Hillary Clinton if Emin was friends with Donald Trump and apparently supported him. After attempting to explain my reasoning to him more than a few times, I think he finally grew tired of my answer: that politics had nothing to do with it, and this was merely a potential promotional opportunity for Emin.

As the day dragged on, so did the questioning. There were some attempts to link me to other obscure Russian "connections." I was asked about my work as publicist for the Russian Tea Room and if it had questionable associations. This iconic restaurant has been a mainstay in New York City for more than ninety years, and fortunately appeared very familiar to at least one of the members of this committee, New York Congressman Peter King, who I am sure had dined there on many occasions.

I wondered why all of these separate government committees couldn't just join forces and either send representatives to one giant hearing, or share the testimony between themselves. After all, most of the questions and topics appeared virtually identical.

I understood that they had a job to do, and justice needed not only to be done, but to be seen to be done. Eventually, after more than seven hours of questioning, the session finally ended. Now

I was free to return home, not to New York, but to my second home, Bangkok, and continue with the last few weeks of my gap year.

As I was escorted through the main lobby of the Capitol, it seemed unreal to me that I had just given testimony on Capitol Hill to members of Congress, discussing the President of the United States, his relationship with Russia, his relationship with me and my client, and my supposed role as the middleman.

A lifetime of reporting and working in the world of entertainment and music promotion had left me with the firm conviction that nothing could shock me. But I was wrong. This few days in the seat of America's government had done just that.

Next time I would return to Washington, I knew I would face the biggest challenge yet: an interview with Robert Mueller's Special Counsel team and a grand jury appearance.

Chapter 19

1600 Pennsylvania Avenue

I spent Christmas and New Year's in Bangkok with friends who had flown in to Thailand from the UK and Australia for their end of year holidays. It was something we had all done for almost two decades, and it was comforting and fun to see them all after such a crisis-filled year. I met with friends around the pool at the majestic Oriental Hotel, went shopping at MBK and Paragon Malls, and ate dinner in my favorite quirky restaurants like Eat Me, Cafe des Stagiaires, and Never Ending Summer. I went back to my routine of visiting Thai temples, taking boat rides down the *Chao Praya* river, and ending the day with trips to chaotic late-night food and flower markets. All of this was made better by the abundance of hour-long foot massages.

I tried to forget the hearings I had just completed in Washington and, more importantly, tried not to think about those that still awaited me the following month. I was scheduled for another trip to Washington for the all-important meeting with special counsel Robert Mueller's investigators, as well as an appearance in front of the daunting grand jury.

To use a famous phrase from Britain's Queen Elizabeth after one of her most difficult years, this had indeed been my *annus horribilis.* I couldn't wait for 2017 to end, so I could close this chapter of my life. At the same time I wondered, with mixed emotions, what 2018 would bring.

Even what I thought would be the last few days of peace and quiet would not go according to plan.

On my final Saturday in Bangkok, I had some last-minute errands to do before packing for my return home. I went to pay some bills to close out accounts at my rented apartment, including an electric bill, which had vastly reduced in cost since I finally worked out, after six months, how to live without twenty-four hour air conditioning. I headed over to the nearby 7-Eleven to pay it, which is how you pay your electric bill in Thailand. Realizing I was low on cash, I stopped first at the ATM in front of the store as I had done countless times during the past six months. I put my US bank debit card into the machine and followed the prompts.

Thai ATMs can be a little temperamental, so I didn't think much of it when the screen read: "Declined by bank." I tried again. And got the same response. I switched to my business debit card from the same bank, tried again, and waited for the crisp Thai baht notes to be dispensed. But once again came the "Declined by bank" message. I began to sweat, and not just because of the afternoon's scorching sun. Something was wrong with my accounts, and I was thousands of miles away.

I knew there was enough money in my account to cover the amount I had requested. Then an alarm went off in my head. Was my bank account frozen or even closed as part of the ongoing RussiaGate investigation?

It seemed illogical, especially after I had so recently spent three days giving testimony as a voluntary witness, telling three committees everything I knew. So much of what had happened to me of late made no sense, so it seemed at least worth investigating. At this point I was without cash and unable to access funds, and there was still almost a week to go before I would return to New York City. There was also the very urgent need to pay the remaining outstanding bills at my rented Bangkok apartment.

I headed back home and logged on to my online banking. To my horror, my account information did not appear at all. The funds had seemingly vanished. It was as if the account had never existed. David also tried to use his card from the same bank and discovered his accounts were closed. This was a major problem. I was thousands of miles away and suddenly penniless, and to top it all off it was the weekend, so banks in the US would no doubt be operating with a skeleton staff.

I managed to speak to a customer service representative who, although polite, said that he could not (or perhaps would not) be able to tell me what had happened to my missing accounts. He did assure me that the money was safe and was still with the bank, but that I did not have access to those accounts any longer. It made no sense to me. He urged me to wait a few hours until my branch was open, and assured me that they should be able to explain what had happened and what the next steps were.

After that, I really started to panic. I had six more days in Thailand and then three more scheduled in Tokyo en route to New York, and yet I was unable to access a single dollar in cash from any of my bank accounts. There was still almost four hours before my own bank branch in New Jersey opened for business. I spent much of that time googling possible reasons for the sudden disappearance of my funds.

There appeared to be only three possible scenarios: the accounts had been frozen by an entity such as the FBI or the IRS (in which case, it would take weeks and perhaps months before the accounts might be unfrozen); or my accounts had been closed by the bank, who no longer wanted me as a customer; or my accounts had been hacked through fraudulent activity.

I didn't think I'd been hacked. Logically, if it was an issue with a government agency, it would most likely mean I would be unable to resolve the problem quickly. If it was a bank issue, I would need to be in the US, and I wouldn't be there for another week.

I finally got hold of someone at my bank who informed me that indeed my accounts were no longer active and had been officially closed by the bank. They were unable to give me a reason over the phone, adding that a letter had been sent to me in advance of the closing, which advised me of their decision to terminate the accounts. Because I had been living overseas for months, I never received it.

When I pointed this out, the bank representative agreed to reopen my checking account for just a few days to enable me to access sufficient funds to get myself back to the US. There, I would need to come into the branch immediately to close the accounts in person. They never gave me a reason why they were terminating my accounts.

As a result, my first few days back in the US were hectic—closing my accounts, opening new ones, and moving back into the apartment I had rented out the previous summer when I had first set forth on my relaxing, rejuvenating gap year. I kept thinking I was going to get my life back and I kept discovering that I was still like a cork bobbing on the sea of a huge scandal.

I decided to go to Washington a day early in order to focus my mind and prepare for my session before Mueller's team. I checked into the JW Marriot Hotel and went out for lunch. It started to snow but I decided to walk back to my hotel despite the bitter cold. Then it occurred to me that I had no idea where my hotel was actually located. I had used an Uber to get to the restaurant, and although it appeared nearby, I had completely forgotten the address. I knew I was close, so I decided to ask a traffic cop standing nearby.

"I know this sounds odd," I said to him, "but I can't remember where I live."

He was keen to help and asked me where I thought I lived. "I think it's 1600 Pennsylvania Avenue," I told him.

He looked surprised. "Come again?" he replied.

"I am pretty sure I'm staying at 1600 Pennsylvania Avenue," I said, feeling confident I had at least remembered the address.

This time his expression changed. "I don't think you do live there. That's the White House."

Now it was my turn to look surprised, as I quickly told him I was pretty certain that the JW Marriott was located at that address.

"I think you will find that your hotel is actually closer to 1300 Pennsylvania Avenue," said the cop, looking at me strangely as the snow continued to fall.

"Yes, you are correct," I blurted out, thanking him and beating a hasty retreat.

It was not a good sign. I couldn't even remember the address of a hotel I had checked into less than two hours earlier, and yet tomorrow I would be expected to remember detail after detail of events that had happened years ago.

I also couldn't help thinking what would have happened if that cop had decided to ask me for ID and perhaps recognized my name. I had visions of the next day's newspaper headlines: "British-Born Publicist Rob Goldstone Says He Lives in The White House!"

Chapter 20

Mueller, Me & the Grand Jury

Although I had seen and heard much about the special counsel's investigation, I really had no idea what to expect. I was pretty certain that at least the partisan rhetoric of the previous meetings wouldn't be present at this one, which would hopefully result in a more straightforward line of questioning.

For some reason I expected that my interview would take place in the FBI's imposing J. Edgar Hoover Building, which I had passed many times on numerous visits to Washington. Instead, it would take place in a characterless office building downtown.

It had been arranged that I would be picked up outside my hotel by FBI agents in an unmarked car and driven to the interview. This was so that I could avoid the always-present TV cameras positioned at the entrance to their building. I appreciated the gesture—the idea of facing the media was almost as anxiety-inducing for me as facing the investigation itself. It was only a short ride to the location, and we entered the office building via an underground garage.

I was escorted into a waiting elevator and introduced to the attorney from Mueller's team who would lead the questioning.

We entered a small windowless room, where he was joined by a handful of colleagues from the Department of Justice and the FBI. There were far fewer people at this meeting than at the hearings, and as their questioning developed, I felt much more at ease with them than I had with the Senate and House Committees. The session turned out to be methodical, logical and reassuringly straightforward.

Much of what they asked me I had already covered in the previous interviews. Naturally, they asked about my email to Don Jr.; they asked about the Trump Tower meeting; and they even asked about the favor I had done for my Muppet friend at VK. Additionally, from time to time they asked if I had ever met or known individuals that appeared to be on some kind of list—mostly with unfamiliar, mainly Russian-sounding names. I was thankful that I hadn't met and didn't know any of those people.

They asked me many questions about the Agalarov's additional requests for meetings for Veselnitskaya with the Trump campaign. When pressed by the special counsel attorney as to why I thought Trump's office hadn't responded to the later requests for a meeting, I explained that I was so horrified at being asked to set up another Trump Tower meeting with this same absurd cast of characters that I used every excuse and delaying tactic I could come up with, to stall the inevitable. I told them that I eventually only made the formal request around Thanksgiving, when I was pretty certain it would get overlooked or lost in the chaos of the holiday period—which apparently it did.

After a full day of questioning, the Mueller session came to an end. It was a huge relief to have gotten through such a stressful meeting with seemingly no major obstacles. I had even brought some light relief during the quick lunch break by telling the group how I had mistakenly told the DC cop that I lived at the White House.

I had been advised before this interview that most likely I would be asked to recount my testimony at a later date to the grand jury, once a mutually agreed time could be found. The grand jury, I was told, usually only met on Fridays, and the requirement for me to appear was indeed confirmed once the interview here was completed and I was getting ready to leave.

I knew that one major difference between all the previous interviews and the grand jury is that I would have to face giving testimony alone. Attorneys for witnesses are not admitted to grand jury hearings. My attorneys could accompany me to the grand jury session, but would have to stay in a waiting room outside while I testified on my own. Additionally, grand jury testimony is sworn under oath. I was well aware of that implication. I had seen and read reports of people being indicted because they had given inconsistent facts, or had flat out lied to a grand jury. I had no intention of doing either, but it was still a scary prospect.

This would be one occasion when I prayed that my memory wouldn't fail me. Even though this would hopefully be my final testimony in this entire investigation, it would definitely be the most nerve-wracking.

As sorry as I felt for myself, I felt just as sorry for the twenty-three members of the public who had already been serving on this grand jury for months with no end in sight. I would hopefully be there only for a few hours, whereas I had heard that the members of this particular grand jury might have to sit for up to eighteen months.

A few weeks later, I found myself back in Washington and ready to face this final hurdle. Once again, the same two FBI agents picked me up in an unmarked car at my hotel; we drove to yet another nondescript office building, parked in an underground garage and were frisked by TSA-style security personnel before getting into a freight elevator to reach our final destination.

I knew the media would be furious that they had somehow missed my arrival. For weeks many of them had been emailing me each Friday morning asking if this was the day I would meet with the grand jury. They would have to keep guessing.

Within a few minutes of arriving, I was shown into the jury room. It was a surreal feeling to enter this secret gathering.

I had been told that there are three levels of differentiation for those appearing before a grand jury. You can be the target of an investigation, the subject of an investigation, or appear simply as a witness. I was there as a voluntary witness. There had been no suggestion or need for any kind of subpoena as far as I was concerned. From the start, I had always made it clear that I was willing and ready to meet and testify in a voluntary capacity with all the inquiry teams, and hopefully this was the last.

As I took my seat opposite the grand jury, I looked out to see the faces of those who would be listening to my testimony. They were a diverse group of men and women, young and old, black and white, all seated lecture-style on three separate tiers.

The room was more like a classroom than a courtroom. It was stuffy and windowless, with an overhead projector and a screen and a couple of desks. There were piles of papers on the attorneys' desks, while my desk was empty except for a bottle of water and my reading glasses. A court reporter sat to my right, ready to notate every word I uttered.

I was asked to swear an oath and state my name for the record. As I began to speak, I could feel what I knew was a panic attack beginning. I started to sweat and my mouth was dry. I was glad I had brought my own large bottle of water and quickly took a few gulps. I began to fiddle with my spectacles in the hope it would distract me long enough to avoid what appeared to be the start of a full-blown anxiety attack. I hadn't had one in over twenty years, but I still remembered the feeling like it was yesterday.

These attacks had started during my years working at HMV, when I used to dread large corporate meetings and making presentations at them. At one point these attacks got so bad that I had to stop driving and have rarely gotten behind the wheel of a car since. I also liked to avoid huge crowds, as well as confined spaces, wherever possible, as these had also been my triggers.

Since then, I had taught myself how to avoid and, more importantly, how to stop a panic attack once it had begun. I took medication to keep them under control, but for years I had not experienced any symptoms. This grand jury appearance, it seemed, had triggered all my past anxieties, and I could feel myself going into a full-fledged episode. I knew that I urgently needed to shake it off if I was to get through what was possibly going to be the most stressful day of my life.

The Mueller team consisted of two attorneys: the same well-spoken man who had questioned me previously, and a woman who I had not met before. They began the hearing by passing me the first of dozens of documents to comment on. The need to concentrate on every single word printed on these individual sheets of paper was exactly what I needed at that moment to take my mind off my anxiety.

Slowly, I began to notice the cold sweaty feeling begin to subside, and I knew that my trusted technique was working. Now I just had to concentrate one hundred percent on the questions I was being asked and ignore any anxious thoughts.

For the next few hours I diligently examined document after document, and answered dozens of questions on a range of subjects all related to Trump and/or Russia in some way or another. While many of the questions were familiar to me, there was something about the setting that made me answer every detail with the utmost care and attention. My greatest fear was that I would go blank or make a mistake that appeared as an inconsistency. It was not, I suppose, a totally reasonable fear, since I had testified four times about this material already, but anxiety is not a reasonable emotion.

Every so often, I would glance over and study the faces of the grand jury members. While most appeared interested in, and indeed curious about, what I had to say, a couple of them appeared to nod off from time to time, and one woman even had a large blanket pulled up all the way to her chin. This seemed odd as I was still sweating, but maybe that was nerves and not the temperature in the room.

After a session lasting just a little under four hours, I was done. Somehow, I had managed to survive my first (and hopefully last) appearance before a grand jury. It hadn't been quite as terrifying as I had imagined when I first sat down, and the jury members asked for only a few points of clarification. I took that as a positive sign that my testimony at least had been clear and to the point.

They had even smiled when I recounted my stories of Trump in his office with his rap music platinum disc, and how Trump and Putin never got to meet because the king of Holland was late.

As crazy as it may sound, for a brief moment I felt conflicted that this hadn't been an actual trial. If it were, I was sure the jurors would have returned a "not guilty" verdict had I been defending my role in all of this, and then I would have been able to finally close this chapter of my life forever. Fortunately for me, however, I was not on trial. Still, as a witness I had been told that I could, at any time in the future, be called to testify in a trial should prosecutors deem me useful to their case.

The gray cloud that had hung over my head for almost a year, therefore, would continue to hover indefinitely, and I would return to New York knowing that the future was uncertain as long as this investigation continued.

It seemed to be only a hint of what Emin had called "blue sky" ahead. All I could do was look toward it and hope for the best.

Chapter 21

Got Me Good

For months after the hearings, I stayed well under the radar in New York and, for the most part, went fairly unrecognized apart from occasional double-takes by my neighbors. Their reactions to seeing me back home could best be summed up in one of two ways: a look of sadness and pity, as if I were suffering from one of those hard-to-pinpoint diseases and they wanted to show sympathy but didn't quite know how; or a look of startled amazement as if I had died and now had miraculously come back to life, like Frankenstein's monster.

But while these encounters were awkward, they were nothing compared to what happened one Saturday afternoon in the summer of 2018. I was standing and chatting with friends in front of my building before heading into the city. After I got into a friend's car, a large, stocky, well-dressed man approached my window, which was rolled down. In a vitriolic rage, he began to scream, "You're the faggot who set up that Trump Tower meeting! Fuck you, you fucking faggot!" I was speechless, and for a second it looked like he was going to try to pull me out of the vehicle.

I urged my friends to drive away quickly. They were horrified, and although I tried to brush it off to somehow lessen the shock of what had just happened in front of them, it was deeply frightening. The entire incident was captured by my apartment building's security cameras, and when I watched it back, it was clear that if we had not driven off when we did, the confrontation could have escalated into something much more serious. I was advised to report the incident to the police, possibly as a hate crime because of the language used, but in the end I decided not to. I couldn't face the possibility of more unwanted media attention.

Until the car incident, attacks had mostly come via emails, texts, and Twitter comments. By far the most disturbing of these for me were a series of hate-filled phone messages left for me by someone who I had known as a friend in the entertainment industry for almost twenty years. His vicious tirade included the hope that I would "get what was coming" to me as "traitor" to the United States, and that I was an outcast in the music and entertainment industry. Most shocking was that this so-called friend equated his uncontrollable hatred of Trump with an uncontrollable hatred of me. In his mind, we had become one and the same.

Returning to work also proved more challenging than I had anticipated. As a publicist, my professional life had revolved around my relationship with the press. But because I had chosen to remain isolated, refusing to talk with the media, my job was now impossible. Instead of being able to pitch my clients to newspapers or TV, writers and producers were only interested in talking about me. I soon realized that I'd become one of the things I had always hated the most in my industry: a publicist who got more attention than his clients.

When I first began managing Emin, I had, out of necessity, let most of my clients go. There simply wasn't enough time to manage him and handle PR or produce events. My schedule was just too unpredictable and I could never be sure what country I'd be in from week to week. With Emin now gone, I needed to find new accounts in order to survive financially. Going after work was something I had always enjoyed, but now it was much more complicated. When I pitched myself, I had to be upfront about the situation I was in.

It was a lot to take in and tricky to maneuver, and some people, understandably, felt unsure about the perceived association, no matter how much they liked me personally. They were concerned that by hiring me, they would somehow be drawn into the murky world of RussiaGate, or find their business under some government spotlight. I understood their concerns and told them so.

There was also the matter of the few clients still associated with my company. They needed reassuring that all was well. The first of these was the Friars Club. Not only was I technically still their publicist, but I was also a Friar myself. They had made me a member years before, and I was delighted to be part of this iconic entertainment institution.

Before I had left for my gap year, I had promised the Friars that I would fly back from Asia to handle PR for their next celebrity Roast. As it happened, that Roast was suddenly canceled. The celebrity Roastee in question was Harvey Weinstein.

After my return to New York, I had lunch at the Friars Club with its executive director to discuss upcoming projects. When the subject of their next Roast came up, there was a new complication. The Friars had decided to honor legendary women's rights campaigner and attorney Gloria Allred. I told him I thought this was a great idea and would certainly get good press coverage.

There was just one problem. He told me that one name being floated as Allred's potential special guest of honor was none other than Hillary Clinton. I almost choked on my club sandwich. I quickly suggested that he needed to broach the subject of me handling PR for the event with Allred and the team organizing the Roast. I told him that while I would be delighted to be involved, I already knew what the answer would be.

"There's no way she'll agree to it," I said, explaining how I believed that photographers wouldn't be able to resist snapping pictures of Hillary Clinton, not next to feminist champion Gloria Allred but alongside Trump Tower email writer Rob Goldstone.

A few days later he called to tell me that I wouldn't be handling PR for the event, even though in the end I heard nothing of Hillary Clinton having attended. I wondered how many more high profile events might prove awkward for me. Thankfully, the Friars had already honored Donald Trump years ago, so at least that potentially wobbly bridge had already been crossed.

While some people had interpreted the social media images and videos of me with clients or working events as evidence that I loved the limelight and the trappings of showbiz, that was just perception. What many failed to understand was it is my job, and a job, I believe, I do well. It's similar to pictures on Facebook or Instagram. They all look pretty fabulous, but they're only snapshots of heightened reality. They're fun, but they're not real life. There's also an irony in what I do that most people are unaware of. Nowhere in life is someone as invisible as they are when they're working a red carpet. Hundreds of eyes might be facing forward, but not one of them is looking at the publicist.

I'd spent decades seeking attention for others, and had always been very aware of what that attention brought—and have never wanted any part of it. I always said I'd rather be Simon Fuller, the man who created *American Idol* and lived in relative anonymity, than Simon Cowell, whose worldwide fame meant he was recognized wherever he went. I didn't want to be judged on my appearance; judged if I chose to wear a silly hat; or judged if I chose to make absurd videos for my friends.

One of those friends summed up my situation clearly when he said that although I hadn't asked for the cards I'd been dealt over the past twelve months, I had to accept them and figure out how to move on. I am, at least for the time being, no longer an anonymous working publicist, but, I suppose, a media figure of sorts.

In July 2018, Emin released a music video for his new single "Got Me Good." I'd heard vague rumors that he was planning some kind of satirical video about RussiaGate, but still it came as a surprise. It had a cast of lookalike characters that included Donald Trump, Stormy Daniels, Hillary Clinton, Ivanka Trump, Kim Jong-Un, and even Facebook founder Mark Zuckerberg.

The video appeared to be shot in the Ritz Carlton Hotel in Moscow, the same hotel where Donald Trump had stayed during the Miss Universe pageant, and the same hotel where the alleged "pee tape" was supposedly filmed. In the video, there were bikini-clad pageant contestants, briefcases being exchanged, and lots of surveillance and spying. Front and center of the video were the words "Fake News."

It was obvious to me what Emin was attempting to convey, but for many people the message appeared both confused and confusing. Within hours of its release, more than a dozen journalists reached out to me asking what the video meant. They wanted to know about its symbolism. They wanted to know if the release date had significance. They wanted to know if there were hidden messages in the lyrics, and were particularly intrigued by Emin singing to the lookalike Donald Trump: "Wish you at least could be honest; I wish that you told me the truth." They asked if Emin was hinting that Trump had lied about something.

I explained to them that I hadn't worked with Emin in over a year and couldn't say for sure what his intention was with the new video. In fact, I had seen it online at exactly the same time they had. Unsurprisingly, the headlines came in rapid succession:

"Collusion-linked Russian pop star mocks Trump in music video" (*New Republic*); "The Russian pop star Emin Agalarov just dropped an insane music video trolling Trump, Clinton, Facebook, and Stormy Daniels" (*Business Insider*); "Watch the Russian Singer Linked to Trump Tower Meeting Troll Mueller in Music Video" (*Observer*); "Russian pop star with ties to Trump trolls U.S. election saga in music video" (AP); "Russian singer tied to Trump campaign trolls everyone with 'Pee Tape' music video" (*The Wrap*); and "Emin Agalarov, Trump-Connected Russian Pop Singer, Trolls The World With New Video" (NPR).

The headlines reminded me of my experience over the past year. Each outlet was watching the same video, but interpreting the intention and meaning a little differently. The press was trying to make sense out of something that, frankly, didn't make sense. It wasn't just a flawed narrative and execution, it was a muddled concept. To my mind, the only thing the video clearly conveyed was a glimpse into the frenetic, contradictory, ever-changing world of Emin.

The following day, Emin appeared on ABC's *Good Morning America* in a satellite interview with host George Stephanopoulos, who hammered him with questions, not only about the video, but also about RussiaGate and the Trump Tower meeting. The ABC host wanted answers.

"Why did you tell Rob Goldstone to contact Don Jr.?" Stephanopoulos pointedly asked.

Emin appeared irritated and responded stiffly: "George, the thing is, there is a criminal investigation currently going on, and I think more than one. So I think it would be inappropriate for me to—to comment on that."

But Stephanopoulos would not give up so easily and again asked, "But you did—you did direct Rob Goldstone to try to set up that meeting, correct?"

Again Emin sidestepped the question by saying he felt it wasn't appropriate to comment on an ongoing investigation.

I had hoped Emin would use the interview to shed light on what he'd failed to explain when he asked me to contact the Trumps and set up the meeting in the first place. Frustratingly, that didn't happen, and the interview ended with no one, including me, being any the wiser.

The day before, however, was decidedly different. Emin finally revealed in an interview with HBO's *VICE News* that he had, in fact, spoken to Don Jr. by phone prior to the meeting, as I had always believed. According to Emin, this is when Don Jr. agreed to the meeting. As Emin recalled, "Don Jr. said, 'Of course. I'll do it [take the meeting] if you're asking.'" So it was now clear, Don Jr. had agreed to the Trump Tower meeting not because of my email, but because Emin had asked him directly.

In his Senate Judiciary Committee testimony, Don Jr. had testified that there had been "no way to gauge the reliability, credibility, or accuracy" of what I wrote to him. But it wasn't the wording or contents of my email that got him to take the meeting. What I wrote was intended to get his attention which it did. But like me, my email was only a conduit for something else: the call. Don Jr.'s conversation with Emin appears to be what had sealed the deal.

Like most aspects of the meeting and the Trump Tower scandal, there has been enormous speculation and confusion over my relationship with the Trumps. It has been characterized as everything from a "casual acquaintance," to a "colleague," "business associate," and even "close family friend." In truth, it was never any of those things. I have met Donald Trump a handful of times and Don Jr. only twice before the Trump Tower meeting—always in a business capacity, and always as a representative of the Agalarovs. When Don Jr. spoke of taking the meeting as a favor to an "acquaintance," it was widely assumed that acquaintance was me. I always believed he was referring to Emin.

During one of the most difficult times of the past year, at a time when I wasn't smiling a whole lot, a friend of mine lightened my mood when he joked that history might ultimately have a different view of my role in RussiaGate.

"You know, if your email ends up helping bring down Trump, you'll probably be named *Time* magazine's *Man of the Year!*"

It made me laugh. Not because there was any chance of either of those things happening, but because of the absurdity of it all and the fact that life can change beyond recognition in the time it takes to write an email. What seems reasonable and logical one minute can become improbable and menacing the next.

But more than anything else, I'll never quite get over how an email written in three minutes on a cellphone, full of attention-grabbing hyperbole, had so spectacularly and completely Trumped my life.

Author's Acknowledgments

This book could not have been written without David Wilson, who not only lived with me throughout this entire story, but also helped me edit my thoughts and make sense of them all. Without his constant encouragement and advice, there is a good chance this book would contain only blank pages.

Thanks to Andrew Torrey for his incredible cover design idea, and to Francine Mendicino and Ann Irwin for turning that idea into reality.

I am grateful to Peri Muldofsky for her many helpful suggestions, and to David Perozzi for his wisdom, guidance, and occasional wit.

My gratitude to attorneys Bob Gage and Bernard Ozarowski for helping me navigate these unfamiliar and often choppy waters.

To my friends and colleagues in New York, London, and around the globe who have supported me throughout this bizarre ordeal and throughout my life, a huge thank you…you all know who you are.

And finally…a big shout out to my amazingly creative Godson—George W—for always telling it like it is, and for keeping it real. I hope you'll make the movie of this book one day.

"BOBERT"

Rob Goldstone is a British-born journalist, celebrity publicist and music manager.

He began his career as a journalist writing for UK newspapers and venturing into broadcast radio. Goldstone then moved first to Sydney, Australia and later to New York City to pursue a career in marketing, public relations and, ultimately, music management.

For the past two decades Goldstone has been based in New York City although he travels extensively—both for work and pleasure.

He has written countless features and articles, *Pop Stars, Pageants & Presidents: How An Email Trumped My Life* marks his debut as an author.

Lightning Source UK Ltd.
Milton Keynes UK
UKHW041130061118
331808UK00002B/24/P